Eating
With Relish

Eating
With Relish

Kathy Gunst

Illustrations by Keiko Narahashi

Foreword by Ken Hom

A COMET BOOK

To John

A Comet Book Published in 1986
by the Paperback Division of
W.H. Allen & Co. Plc 44 Hill Street, London W1X 8LB

First published in the United States of America by G. P. Putnam's
Sons, 1984

Sweet-and-Sour Red Cabbage Soup reprinted by permission of Sara Moulton.
Jim Fobel's Low-Sodium Mustard reprinted by permission of Jim Fobel.
'Nam Prik' reprinted by permission of The Putnam Publishing Group from *The Original Thai Cookbook* by Jennifer Brennan. Copyright © 1981 by Jennifer Brennan.
Jessica's Pickled Oriental Radishes reprinted by permission of Jessica Weber. Copyright © 1983 by Jessica Weber.
Apple Cider Jelly reprinted by permission of Kate Slate.
Breast of Duck in a Mustard, Orange, Champagne Sauce with Candied Lime Slices and Walnuts reprinted by permission of James Haller, Chef of The Blue Strawberry Restaurant in Portsmouth, New Hampshire.
Quick Ketchup reprinted by permission of Penny Potenz Winship. Copyright © 1983 by Penny Potenz Winship.
Hot-Sweet Mustard reprinted by permission of Anne Montgomery.
Tomato-Apple Relish and Watermelon Rind Pickle reprinted by permission of Connie Weeks from *Using Summer's Bounty* by Connie Weeks.

Typeset by Phoenix Photosetting, Chatham
Printed and bound in Great Britain by
Mackays of Chatham Ltd, Kent

ISBN 0 86379 118 2

Acknowledgments

Thanks to everyone who lent their tastebuds and helped me decipher the good condiments from the bad: Gene Brown, Bill Bell, Sarah Grossman, Barry Cantor, Stanley Dorn, Jeff Rathaus, Jim Haller, Tom O'Brien, Stephanie Curtis, Kate Slate, Mardee Regan, Nancy Rudolph, Lucy Rudolph, Judy Wenning, Connie Weeks, Michael Gunst and Matt Lewis and Shelley Boris from Dean & Deluca.

Thanks to Robert Cornfield, my agent, for all his support, guidance and good ideas and to my editor, Diane Reverand, for believing in this project and giving me lots of good editorial advice.

Many thanks to the producers, manufacturers and cooks who introduced me to their wonderful products.

Thank you to Dorothee Kocks who spent long hours typing this manuscript and giving me positive feedback at a time when I really needed it.

Thank you to the editors at *Diversion* magazine who published my first article (on mustard) some seven years ago, and to the people at *Food & Wine* magazine for all their support and encouragement.

Also, thanks to Nancy and Lee Gunst and Leona and Leonard Levy who thought the idea of leaving college for a year and going off to cooking school wasn't so crazy after all.

And finally, thanks to Karen Frillmann for being a friend through it all and to John Rudolph, who loves condiments more than anyone else I know.

Foreword

The secret of good food involves many elements: a knowledge of cooking techniques, a good palate, the best and freshest ingredients and finally an understanding of condiments which help to flavour the food to make a dish complete.

When I first met Kathy, many years ago, I was impressed by her knowledge of foods and was therefore thrilled to read her book of condiments. Now with Kathy's expert guidance you can sift through all the multiple assorted condiments which are increasingly available throughout the UK. She is authoritative without being boring. I like the straightforward manner in which the book has been organised. It is full of information and I find myself constantly reaching for it as a source of reference. The recipes here are simple and delicious. What more can anyone want from a food book?

This book is certainly an important asset in any cook's arsenal. Use it with gusto and enjoy the wide world of condiments through the eye, palate, nose and words of an expert cook who cares.

Ken Hom

Contents

Introduction

CONDIMENTS ARE TO FOOD what jewellery and make-up are to clothing. They are not essential; they won't keep you warm or well fed, but they definitely 'dress up' your food and make eating a lot more interesting.

What exactly is a condiment? Mustard, chutney, relish and hot pepper sauce are condiments. But so are many oils and vinegars. Of course you can cook with an extra virgin olive oil or an aged wine vinegar, but these items are at their best when they are used to embellish other dishes. And it is this ability, to complement the flavours in other foods, that distinguishes a condiment from a herb, spice or other raw ingredient.

Up until a few years ago, the only condiments you found in most people's kitchens were mayonnaise, ketchup and bright yellow mustard. But recently the list has grown: Dijon mustard, Italian olive oil and Japanese soy sauce have also become basic items. What most people don't realise is that there are hundreds of other wonderful condiments that can be bought or made. The whole point of this book is to help you to discover them.

Have you ever tried a home-made peach chutney, laced with ginger, spices and peppers, served with a spicy lamb curry? Or a Moroccan chilli pepper sauce grilled on oysters; an oil made from the essence of hazelnuts sprinkled over a mixed green salad; or soy sauce, garlic, spring onions and lime juice served as a dipping sauce with deep-fried prawns?

Of course, condiments can also be served with simpler foods. A grainy mustard on a hot dog, home-made ketchup on a hamburger or pickled watermelon rind served with a sandwich. Condiments were originally created thousands of years ago to improve the flavour of everyday foods. The beauty of condiments is that they can make eating the same foods every day seem like a completely new experience each time.

In the last few years condiments have become 'hot' items in speciality food shops and the larger supermarkets. You can now choose from literally hundreds of mustards, oils, vinegars, chutneys, relishes, sauces and jellies from round the world. But should you indulge in a jar of fancy, imported mustard? Is it any

9

better than the mustard you've been using for the past ten years? Is a bottle of extra virgin olive oil worth the price? The answer is yes, but only if you know which ones to buy and how to use them.

Over the last year I've tasted hundreds of different condiments. I've given hints for how to use these, recipes for cooking with them and, in many cases, recipes for making your own.

Making home-made condiments is very easy. Towards the end of the summer, when fruits, vegetables and herbs are abundant and inexpensive, I spend an entire day making chutneys, ketchups, relishes and pickles. Then in December, when everyone is going crazy trying to decide what to buy for Christmas, I take these condiments out of the store cupboard, put a home-made label on them and cover the jars with decorative fabric and ribbon. An old-fashioned preserving jar filled with coconut chutney, a tall wine bottle of champagne vinegar with garden herbs, or a glass jar packed with an onion and cassis relish are some of the nicest gifts you can give.

By now you've probably realised that this is not a traditional cookbook. It's not a book that asks you to learn new techniques or cooking styles or to spend a lot of money. It is a book that asks you to be creative and a little bit adventurous with the foods you eat. I hope that the suggestions, ideas and recipes you find on the following pages will inspire you to create your own dishes and will help you use condiments to make eating a more pleasurable experience.

Kathy Gunst
South Berwick, Maine
January 1984

1

Mustard

'MY PANTRY IS FILLED with more than 200 mustards and my work has just begun . . .'

I found this sentence in a notebook I entitled 'Mustard Tasting Notes: 1982.' It was written in a state of confusion and anxiety. Every time I thought I was getting to grips with the mustard market, it seemed to grow out from under me. At least once a week someone would call to announce that he or she had just discovered a new mustard that I simply had to taste to believe.

If you've looked into a speciality food shop (or even your local supermarket) lately, you will know exactly what I'm talking about. What was once a simple matter of choosing between four or five different mustards is now a complex, multinational decision. There are now so many mustards on the market that you could spend months tasting them all, trying to decide which ones have the best flavour and which are actually worth the often outrageous price.

The fact is that in recent years mustard has grown more in popularity than any other condiment or spice. There has been a deluge of fancy imports. And mustard makers – both corporate ones and smaller cottage industries – have also reacted to the craze. According to the research of one manufacturer, 'an increasing number of homes are now stocking more than one kind of mustard.'

The variety of mustards available today is matched only by the number of theories about the origin of this spicy brown paste. Mustard seeds can be traced back as far as 3000 BC. The ancient Egyptians, Greeks, Indians and Romans are all said to have grown mustard seeds and cooked the tender leaves of the mustard plant. (The Egyptians originally chewed the seeds whole while eating meat in order to give their food more flavour.) Mustard was eventually brought to Europe, where its popularity flourished. By the thirteenth century, 'Mustarder' was a common occupation.

How mustard found its name is another hotly debated question. In classical times, mustard was made by mixing the pounded seeds with *mustum* (unfermented wine). The suffix '-ard' is supposedly derived from the Teutonic -*hart*, meaning hard, strong or intense – all characteristics of a good mustard. Another explanation is that the word 'mustard' comes from the Latin *mustum ardens*, meaning 'burning must,' since mustard seeds were mixed with grape must in France long ago.

A more romantic story is told by the people of Dijon, France. Long associated with fine mustard, the Dijonnais claim the word was established in the late part of the fourteenth century by Philip the Bold, the Duke of Burgundy. Local legend has it that the Duke had difficulty digesting meat during the lengthy and elaborate banquets he was so famous for giving. He asked his chef to devise a sauce that would disguise the meat's often rancid smell and taste. *Moult ma tarde*, meaning 'a long time I delay my meal,' was the term given to this spicy yellow condiment which allowed the Duke and his guests to savour their food. Later, this phrase was shortened to *moutarde*, the French word for mustard.

This story, apocryphal or not, gives some clue as to why mustard has remained so popular over the centuries. In the past, mustard was enjoyed simply because everyday foods weren't flavourful enough or had a downright bad taste. Early mustard users were not 'gourmets'. Today, despite its association with the 'gourmet' and 'speciality' food world, mustard is loved for similar reasons. Of all condiments, it is undoubtedly the most basic, capable of complementing and enhancing just about every type of savoury food.

MUSTARD SURVEY

Our growing enthusiasm for mustard has produced an onslaught of new products and, not surprisingly, the results are varied. For each terrific new mustard I've tasted, there have been at least five 'duds'. I refer to these mustards as the 'trendies' – mustards that are brimming with interesting ingredients but have absolutely no memorable qualities. Usually these trendies are packaged so beautifully that you'd be willing to bet money that they'll taste good; they just *look* so delicious. But looks can be deceptive. One spoonful and it's all over.

When tasting a mustard, the first thing I look for is pure mustard flavour – not salt, flour, oil or a strong herb taste, but mustard. After all, that's supposedly what you're buying. Far too many of the products I sampled were filled with ingredients that overwhelmed, or conflicted with, the natural flavour of the mustard seeds.

What follows is an attempt to make sense of the ever-growing selection of mustards. I've divided the mustards into nine major types and given some hints on what they'll go best with.

American-Style Mustard

The word 'style' in this category is significant. Although there is now a large (and impressive) selection of American mustards to choose from, what is truly defined as American-style mustard is *not* terribly impressive. But, like iceberg lettuce, American-style mustard has its place.

Everyone in the United States knows about this type of mustard. Its mild (some would say bland) taste and bright yellow colour is a familiar childhood memory. In the midst of raving about all the new, exotic mustards on the market, we tend to forget about old favourites.

American-style mustard breaks down into two basic categories: the smooth, bright yellow 'ball park' mustard made from ground white seeds, vinegar, sugar and spices (most notably turmeric, a deep-yellow-coloured spice used in curries); and the coarser, somewhat spicier brown 'deli-style' mustard, made from a mixture of ground white and black seeds, vinegar and spices.

TASTING NOTES:
American mustards seem to have been made to be eaten with hot dogs. They are also a good accompaniment to delicatessen sandwiches, sausages and baked beans.

Dijon and Dijon-Style Mustard

As far as I'm concerned, nothing rivals a good Dijon mustard. It should be pungent and spicy with a smooth, creamy texture. The Dijonnais have an expression to describe the characteristics of a truly good mustard: *mont au nez*, meaning 'coming up to the nose'. It is also said in Dijon that mustard should 'stimulate the appetite and aid digestion, but never burn the throat or alter the taste of sauces or dishes'.

The Dijonnais take mustard-making as seriously as some of their fellow Burgundians take wine-making. And there are strict laws in France, some dating back as far as the late 1880s, that govern what can, and cannot, go into a Dijon mustard.

According to French law, a Dijon mustard must be made exclusively from black seeds (*brassica nigra*), salts and spices mixed with either white wine, *verjuice* (the juice of unripened grapes), or vinegar. By law, no sugars, flours, oils, perfumes, colourings or additives may be added. Any mustard that deviates from this traditional recipe must be called Dijon-style. Dijon mustard is made by crushing the hulled seeds into a yellow paste and then mixing them with the liquids and flavourings. The mustard is allowed to stand for three days to allow the heat and flavours to come together and then it is bottled. An average of 57,000 metric tons of Dijon mustard is made every year.

TASTING NOTES:
Of all varieties of mustard, Dijon is probably the most versatile. It's perfect served with steaks, leg of lamb, chicken, boiled beef, cold meats, sausages and fish. Try it as a base for vinaigrettes and use it for cooking; its smooth texture and pungent flavour blend easily into soups, stews and sauces.

English Mustard (Powder)

For centuries, mustard has been a staple of the English kitchen. Thirteenth-century Tudor households were said to consume mustard in enormous quantities. An Earl of Northumberland, who apparently was not unlike the rest of his countrymen, would go through between 160 and 190 gallons of mustard a year.

English mustard powder as we know it today is credited to a woman named Mrs Clements. The story goes that in 1720, she developed a powder that produced a smooth-textured mustard rather than the grainy type that was usual throughout England. What was so revolutionary about her mustard was that she ground the seeds in a mill rather than crushing them with a mortar and pestle, and then she put the mustard flour through a sieve to remove the hulls. Mrs Clements took her 'discovery' from town to town and eventually to London, where it found favour with King George I. Soon mustard powder was made on a commercial basis throughout the country. It was referred to as 'Durham mustard' – a tribute to Mrs Clements' home town.

The popularity of English mustard was furthered in 1814 when a miller named Jeremiah Colman bought a flour and mustard mill in Norwich. His company became so successful that, forty years later, he bought a larger factory in Carrow exclusively for producing his pungent mustard powder. Today, the world-famous Colman's mustard is still made in that same factory.

The English have always preferred mustard in powder form. Made of a blend of ground black and white mustard seeds, wheat flour and spices, English mustard is terrifically hot. To make English mustard, simply add cold water to the powder, just enough to make a somewhat thick paste. It should stand for between ten and thirty minutes to develop full flavour and heat. (The full flavour develops after ten minutes and diminishes after a few hours.) You can also experiment by adding milk, cider, flat beer or herbs. Whatever liquid you choose, make sure it is cold; heat will kill the enzymes that activate the pungency and flavour.

TASTING NOTES:
English mustard is extremely versatile. There is no better accompaniment to roast beef or left-over cold meat. It also makes a tangy glaze for baked ham and goes well with sausages and sharp cheeses. Since mustard powder acts as an emulsifier and preservative, it is often added to home-made mayonnaise; it not only adds a delicious flavour, but also prevents curdling.

Flavoured Mustard

Flavoured mustards are essentially Dijon or Dijon-style mustards with the simple addition of a herb, spice or flavouring. You can buy just about every type of flavoured mustard that you can possibly think of – and some you wouldn't want to. They range from a traditional tarragon-flavoured mustard to more esoteric combinations, such as olives and anchovies or tomatoes, currants and beets.

My feeling about these mustards is that, for the most part, they are overpriced and unnecessary. Why is it that manufacturers feel they can charge so much more for a mustard by simply putting a sprig of fresh tarragon in it? Although some of these mustards do make nice gifts, they are just as easy to make on your own. If, for example, you want a lemon- or lime-flavoured mustard, take some Dijon mustard and add a few teaspoons of fresh lemon or lime juice to taste and some grated zest for extra flavour. (See recipe for flavoured mustard on page 22.)

TASTING NOTES:
- Add a tablespoon of flavoured mustard to a basic oil and vinegar dressing.
- Try adding a touch of flavoured mustard to home-made coleslaw or potato salad.
- Spread flavoured mustard on sandwiches. Some of my favourite combinations include green peppercorn mustard and roast beef; herb-flavoured mustard with chicken or turkey slices; champagne mustard with prawn salad; tarragon-flavoured mustard with chicken salad; and spicy mustard with a toasted cheese sandwich.

- Serve with roast beef, ham, sausages and hamburgers.
- Flavoured mustards add great flavour to grilled steaks, fish and barbecued chicken.
- Mix flavoured mustard with soured cream or yogurt to make a great dip for raw vegetables and grilled prawns.
- Mix a spicy mustard with orange or lemon marmalade and use to glaze spare-ribs, chicken or duck.

German-Style Mustard

The Germans, like the French and the British, adore mustard – or, as they call it, *Senf*. Made from a blend of ground mustard seeds, wine vinegar, salt, sugar and spices, there are two major varieties of German mustard: Bavarian – a sweet, dark mustard; and the more popular Düsseldorf – a spicy mustard similar to Dijon.

TASTING NOTES:
German mustard, it seems, was made to be eaten with sausages and *wurst*. The Düsseldorf mustards, which range from mild to very sharp, stand up to all sorts of spicy sausages and salamis. And there is nothing better served with a steaming platter of sauerkraut, smoked pork and sausages. The sweet flavour of Bavarian mustard complements the more delicate sausages like *Weisswurst*, which is made from veal. German mustards, on the whole, are reasonably priced.

Grainy Mustard

Grainy mustards, or what the French call *moutarde à l'ancienne*, taste like all mustards used to taste before the eighteenth-century innovation of removing the seed's hull. Made from a mixture of ground and semi-ground seeds combined with vinegar and spices, this mustard's greatest asset is its texture. Grainy mustards have a taste similar to Dijon, although they are generally not as sharp. Their texture ranges from somewhat creamy to thick and crunchy.

TASTING NOTES:
- Serve grainy mustards with cold meat platters.
- Use grainy mustards to add flavour and texture to sandwiches.

- Add a tablespoon of grainy mustard to a vinaigrette.
- Spread grainy mustard on a grilled steak, breast of duck or chicken and place under the grill for a mustardy glaze.
- Serve with sautéed liver and onions.
- Serve a selection of grainy mustards with a platter of sweet and hot sausages.
- Add a tablespoon of grainy mustard to a potato and spring onion salad or a home-made prawn salad with orange slices.
- Spread a tablespoon or two of grainy mustard on a thick slice of French or Italian bread and grill. Serve over a bowl of home-made onion, vegetable or pea soup.
- Serve one or two varieties of grainy mustard with a steaming hot dish of home-made corned beef and cabbage.

Hot Mustard

To some people, the key characteristic of good mustard is just how hot it is. Manufacturers, catching on to this 'macho' attitude, have begun producing mustards labelled specifically as 'Hot', 'Super Hot,' etc. Generally, these are Dijon-style mustards with the addition of cayenne pepper, horseradish or chilli peppers.

TASTING NOTES:
These mustards range from mildly spicy to 'Oh-my-God-I-can't-stand-it' hot. Cooking with these mustards isn't always the best idea because they tend to overwhelm other flavours.

Those products marketed specifically as 'Super Hot' are generally all heat and no flavour. My idea of a good hot mustard is a spicy Dijon or a freshly made English or Chinese mustard powder.

Oriental Mustard

Anyone who has ever been to a Chinese restaurant is familiar with *Gai Lot*, the bright yellow, fiery hot mustard that's served with every meal. Made from the very spicy brown seed called *brassica juncea*, it's mustard that can make you feel, if only for a moment, that you'll never, ever, have sinus problems again.

Prepared Chinese mustard is available in jars, but it never seems to have the same impact as the powdered variety. For the real thing, Chinese mustard must be made fresh from equal quantities of ground powder and cold water. Like English mus-

17

tard powder, it should sit for 10–30 minutes to develop full heat and flavour before serving.

Despite popular misconceptions, the hot, pale green stuff that accompanies *sushi*, *sashimi* and many other Japanese dishes is not mustard; it is called *wasabi* and is made from ground green horseradish root (see page 77). There is, however, a Japanese mustard called *karashi*. It's a very strong ground mustard powder that is mixed with water like English mustard powders. *Karashi* is sold in powder form and ready-made in tubes. It is generally used in soy-based dipping sauces and served with dumplings, salads and seafood. Use it sparingly; it's very potent stuff.

TASTING NOTES:

Oriental mustard is traditionally used as a dip with egg rolls or spring rolls. It's also delicious served with dumplings, spare-ribs, Chinese-style steamed fish and noodle dishes.

Sweet Mustard

I have a problem with this type of mustard, since I don't particularly like my mustard sweet. However, it's quite obvious that more than a few people disagree because the number of sweet mustards on the market seems to double every year. The favourite sweetening ingredient is honey, but white sugar, brown sugar and corn syrup are also used. The result is successful only if the basic mustard possesses enough character of its own. Unfortunately, many of these mustards are simply overwhelmed by sweeteners.

The Swedes are extremely fond of sweet mustards. Aside from a few slightly spicy, grainy mustards, the majority of the Swedish mustards that make their way to overseas markets are very sweet.

TASTING NOTES:

These mustards range from slightly sweet to gooey, sickly sweet. Generally, they are not very hot, although there are some mustards that are labelled 'Sweet-Hot'.

Sweet mustards pair particularly well with smoked fish, smoked turkey and smoked meat, like Smithfield ham. The popular Swedish dish *Gravlax* is traditionally served with a sweet mustard-dill sauce. Some people like to mix sweet mustards with soured cream and use as a dip.

MAKING YOUR OWN MUSTARD

Making mustard is a surprisingly straightforward process of grinding and mixing mustard seeds with a few other ingredients. Just what combination of seeds you use, what liquid you choose (water, vinegar, wine, beer, milk, and so forth) and what herbs, spices and flavourings you add determines what sort of mustard you'll end up with.

When making mustard you should realise that the seeds themselves are not hot until they are ground and moistened with some sort of cold liquid. The liquid activates a mixture of enzymes called myrosin, which is what gives the mustard its pungency.

Freshly made mustard is searingly hot. It should be allowed to stand for 10–30 minutes to develop flavour and allow the heat to subside slightly. The longer the mustard stands, the mellower it becomes.

The business of making mustard – both on a commercial basis and at home – invariably involves secrets. Take a look at the labels on a dozen jars of Dijon mustard and you'll see what I mean. Though they all list the same ingredients (mustard seeds, vinegar, salt and spices), they taste very different. It is the manufacturers' special combination of seeds and seasonings that gives each mustard its distinctive flavour.

All mustard comes from the same family, the *cruciferae* plant – so called because it bears flowers with four petals arranged in the shape of a cross. From this plant come three different types of seeds, the basis of all mustard.

The most common is the white seed (*brassica alba*), which is actually a yellowish-tan colour. This is the mildest and is used to make American-style mustards and as a filler with spicier blends. It is also frequently used for making pickles and relishes because of its strong preservative powers.

Brassica nigra or black seed (actually a dark reddish-brown colour) has been known since the earliest times for its potency. Black seeds are far spicier than the white seeds and are used for making hot mustards, most notably those produced in Dijon, France.

The third variety, *brassica juncea* or brown seed, is the hottest of them all. Found throughout the Orient, this seed is said to be so

hot that it actually repels insects while growing. This variety of seed is not generally used in prepared mustards but is frequently used in curries and ground into powder form to make what we call Chinese mustard. It's also used to make mustard oil, a spicy cooking oil sold in shops specialising in Indian foods.

The following home-made mustards should be stored in a glass jar in the refrigerator; they will keep about two to four weeks.

Anne Montgomery's Hot-Sweet Mustard

This mustard is simple to make but needs to stand overnight, so plan accordingly. It has a slightly sweet, spicy flavour. If you don't like your mustard sweet, simply cut the amount of sugar by half. Use on sandwiches, with grilled chicken and sausages.

40 g/1½ oz mustard powder
4 tablespoons white wine vinegar
5 tablespoons dry white wine
1 tablespoon sugar
1 teaspoon salt
2 egg yolks, beaten

In a medium-size bowl, whisk together the mustard powder, vinegar, wine, sugar and salt. Cover and leave to stand overnight. Place the bowl over a pot of simmering water or transfer the mustard to the top of a double boiler. Whisk in the egg yolks and continue whisking until the mustard becomes thick and creamy, about 3–5 minutes. Allow to cool for at least an hour before serving. *Makes about 200 g/7 oz.*

Jim Fobel's Low-Sodium Mustard

If you read their labels, you will notice that most prepared mustards are loaded with salt. This recipe, created by Jim Fobel, author of *Beautiful Food* (Van Nostrand Reinhold), combines mustard seeds with powdered mustard, herbs and other flavourings – without a trace of salt. It's delicious on baked chicken, sandwiches, or as a base for a mustard vinaigrette. This mustard is best prepared the day before.

3 tablespoons yellow mustard seeds
2 tablespoons mustard powder
1½ teaspoons turmeric
1 teaspoon tarragon
¼ teaspoon cinnamon
150 ml/¼ pint water
4 tablespoons plus 2 teaspoons white distilled vinegar
4 tablespoons dry white wine
2 tablespoons sugar
2 tablespoons olive or vegetable oil
1 clove garlic, minced

In a small, heavy stainless steel saucepan, combine the mustard seeds, mustard powder, turmeric, tarragon and cinnamon. Add the water and stir to dissolve the mustard. Bring to the boil over a high heat, stirring constantly. Remove from the heat, cover and leave to stand for 8 hours or overnight.

Add the 4 tablespoons of vinegar, the wine, sugar, oil and garlic and bring to the boil over a high heat. Reduce the heat to low and simmer, stirring frequently, for 5 minutes.

Purée the mustard in a food processor or blender. Transfer to a small bowl and allow to cool to room temperature. Stir in the remaining 2 teaspoons of vinegar and taste for seasoning. If you like your mustard hot, stir in up to one additional teaspoon of mustard powder. Cover and refrigerate for up to two weeks. *Makes about 250 g/9 oz.*

Herb-Flavoured Mustard

I was inspired to create my own herb-flavoured mustard after sampling more than a dozen different bottled varieties which all tasted much too artificial and overbearing. This simple recipe uses a prepared Dijon mustard as its base. It can easily be made with any combination of dried or fresh herbs and herb-flavoured vinegar.

> 100 g/4 oz Dijon mustard
> about 2 teaspoons chopped fresh tarragon, rosemary, basil, thyme, oregano or sage, or 1 teaspoon dried
> about 1 teaspoon tarragon-flavoured vinegar, or any other herb-flavoured vinegar

Place the mustard into a medium-size serving bowl and stir in the herbs and vinegar. Mix well and taste for seasoning. Leave to stand for 10 minutes before serving. *Makes about 100 g/4 oz.*

COOKING WITH MUSTARD

Mustard-Maple Glaze

This recipe provides enough glaze for 4 pork chops or 450 g/1 lb of scallops or prawns. You can also double (or triple) the recipe and use on duck or ham.
Simply add the glaze during the last few minutes of cooking and place the dish under the grill for 2–4 minutes before serving.

3 tablespoons grainy, hot, or Dijon mustard
2½ tablespoons maple syrup
2 tablespoons orange juice
2 teaspoons apple cider

Combine all the ingredients. In a small stainless steel saucepan, bring the glaze to the boil over a high heat. Reduce the heat and let simmer for 5–7 minutes, or until thickened and reduced to about 120 ml/4 fl oz.

Mustard-Cider Cream Sauce

This is a rich, pungent sauce, based on an old Shaker recipe from the Hancock Shaker Village in Massachusetts. It's incredibly good served with smoked fish (particularly trout), ham or roast beef. Make it at least 15 minutes before serving.

175 ml/6 fl oz double cream
40 g/1½ oz brown sugar
2 tablespoons mustard powder
5 tablespoons fresh apple cider
½ tablespoon cider vinegar
pinch of salt
1 egg yolk

Heat 120 ml/4 fl oz of the cream with the sugar in the top half of a double boiler set over barely simmering water (or in a medium-size saucepan set over simmering water) until warm.

In a small bowl, mix the mustard powder, cider, vinegar and salt. Using a whisk, gradually beat the mustard-cider mixture into the warmed cream.

Beat the egg yolk slightly in a small bowl. Add 3 tablespoons of the mustard-cream to the yolk, mix well and gradually add it back to the saucepan. Cook the sauce over a low heat, whisking frequently, for about 5 minutes or until the sauce begins to thicken. Remove from the heat and allow to cool.

Whip the remaining cream until soft peaks form. Gently fold the whipped cream into the mustard and allow to stand for about 15 minutes before serving. *Makes about 350 ml/12 fl oz.*

Scandinavian Mustard-Dill Sauce

Serve this sauce with an assortment of herring, *Gravlax* or smoked fish. It also adds a sweet, pungent flavour to a new potato and chopped spring onion salad.

75 g/3 oz Dijon mustard
2 tablespoons sugar
3 tablespoons white wine vinegar
175 ml/6 fl oz vegetable oil
1½ tablespoons minced fresh dill
salt and pepper to taste

In a small bowl, whisk together the mustard, sugar and vinegar until well blended. Gradually beat in the oil until blended and smooth. Stir in the dill and add salt and pepper to taste. Cover and refrigerate for an hour before serving. *Makes about 250 ml/8 fl oz.*

Mustard Vinaigrette

You can use any type of mustard you want with this vinaigrette; the classic ingredient, however, is Dijon mustard. This dressing is wonderful served over a mixed green salad, over steamed asparagus with a sprinkling of capers and finely chopped hard-boiled egg, or with a simple chicken salad.

1 teaspoon Dijon, grainy or herb-flavoured mustard
3 tablespoons olive oil
2 tablespoons red or white wine vinegar
salt and pepper to taste

Whisk together all the ingredients and serve. *Makes about 5 tablespoons.*

Grilled Salmon with Mustard-Hazelnut Butter

2½ teaspoons hazelnut oil (see page 54)
2 salmon steaks about 4 cm/1½ in thick
25 g/1 oz butter, softened
1 tablespoon grainy or Dijon mustard
1 tablespoon fresh lemon juice
1 tablespoon finely chopped hazelnuts or almonds
(optional)
lemon wedges

Grease a small baking tin or Pyrex dish with 1½ teaspoons of the oil. Place the salmon in the pan and preheat the grill.

In a small bowl, mix the butter, mustard, lemon juice, hazelnuts and remaining 1 teaspoon of oil. Spread the flavoured butter equally on the salmon steaks. Place the salmon about 10 cm/4 in from the heat and grill for 12–15 minutes, or until tender when tested with a fork.

Remove the salmon to a serving plate and spoon the pan juices on top. Serve with roast potatoes or boiled new potatoes. *Serves 2.*

London, 1800

Pork Chops in a Mustard-Cider Sauce

This is a simple, hearty dish that is delicious served with red cabbage and roast or pan-fried potatoes. It can be made more elegant by substituting slices of pork tenderloin (about 4 cm/1½ in thick) for the pork chops.

1 teaspoon olive or vegetable oil
2 cloves garlic, finely minced
2 lean pork chops, centre cut
4 tablespoons Dijon mustard
1 teaspoon sage, crumbled
freshly ground black pepper
250 ml/8 fl oz fresh apple cider

In a medium-size frying pan, heat the oil over a moderately high heat until it begins to get hot. Add the garlic and sauté just until it begins to turn a golden colour. Add the pork chops and brown on both sides.

Raise the heat to high and spread each pork chop with ½ tablespoon of the mustard and ¼ teaspoon of the sage and some pepper. Turn the chops over and repeat. Add half of the cider to the frying pan and let the mixture come to the boil. Reduce the heat to moderate; whisk in a tablespoon of the mustard, and cook for 20–30 minutes, depending on the thickness of the chops, until just cooked and tender, turning frequently. Check to make sure the cider doesn't evaporate completely; add additional cider if necessary.

Raise the heat to high and add the remaining cider. Reduce to a syrupy glaze, turning the pork frequently. Whisk in the remaining tablespoon of mustard, heat and serve. *Serves 2.*

Mustard Butter

Add a tablespoon of this pungent mustard butter to grilled steaks and chops, pan-fried fish and sautéed prawns and oysters.

65 g/2½ oz unsalted butter, at room temperature
1 teaspoon white mustard seeds, slightly crushed
1 teaspoon mustard powder
1 tablespoon dry white wine

¼ teaspoon salt
pinch of freshly ground black pepper

In a small bowl, cream the butter until soft. Add the crushed mustard seeds, mustard powder, wine, salt and pepper and mix until smooth. Place some flour on your hands and shape the butter into a roll or log. Place in waxed paper and refrigerate or freeze until ready to serve. *Makes about 100 g/4 oz.*

Breast of Duck in a Mustard, Orange, Champagne Sauce with Candied Lime Slices and Walnuts

This wonderful dish was created by Jim Haller, a close friend and chef of The Blue Strawberry Restaurant in Portsmouth, New Hampshire. It's perfect for a small dinner party because you can make the sauce and the lime garnish in advance and wait until your guests arrive to cook the duck.

THE SAUCE
100 g/4 oz Dijon mustard
100 g/4 oz grainy mustard
300 g/11 oz orange marmalade
4 tablespoons frozen orange juice concentrate
225 g/8 oz butter, melted
250 ml/8 fl oz dry Champagne, or white wine
1 tablespoon freshly grated nutmeg
50 g/2 oz walnut halves

THE GARNISH
2 limes
250 ml/8 fl oz water
225 g/8 oz caster sugar

THE DUCK
4 duck breasts, about 350–450 g/12 oz–1 lb each

Prepare the sauce: Place all the ingredients for the sauce, except the walnuts, in a blender or food processor and blend until smooth. Place the sauce in a medium-size saucepan and simmer over a moderately high heat for about 30 minutes, or until

27

reduced by one third. Remove the sauce from the heat, stir in the walnuts and set aside.

Prepare the garnish: Thinly slice the limes and place in a medium-size saucepan with the water and the sugar. Simmer over a moderate heat until the lime slices are coated in a thick syrup, about 10 minutes. Leave to stand until ready to serve.

Prepare the duck: Preheat the oven to 240°C/475°F/Gas Mark 9. Place the duck breasts on a rack in a large baking tin. Bake for 20 minutes and remove from the oven. Reduce the heat to 180°C/350°F/Gas Mark 4 and drain off all the fat that has accumulated in the bottom of the pan. Place the duck in the baking tin and cover with some of the sauce. Bake for an additional 15 minutes. Remove from the oven and garnish each duck breast with 2–3 slices of lime. Serve with the additional sauce on the side. *Serves 4.*

Silver Mustard Pot
London, 1782

2

Vinegar

IN JAPAN AND CHINA, vinegar is made from rice wine. In the United States, the main ingredient is apple cider, and in Mexico, cactus leaves or pineapple are used. Throughout Europe, wine and sherry are preferred, and in Sri Lanka, a Buddhist country where alcohol is forbidden, it is made from coconuts.

The word 'vinegar' comes from the French words *vin* and *aigre*, meaning 'soured wine'. When wine, or any other naturally fermented alcohol (such as beer or cider) is exposed to air, it gradually turns to vinegar. The pungent, tart flavour of vinegar has been greatly welcomed by all who have come upon it.

The discovery of vinegar was, in all probability, an accident. Who it was that actually made this discovery is not known, but it surely happened many centuries ago. The Bible is filled with almost as many references to vinegar as it is to wine. The Chinese are known to have made rice wine vinegar over 3,000 years ago. And early drawings show that the Greeks and Romans created elaborate vessels to hold their vinegar into which chunks of crusty bread were dipped.

The business of making and bottling vinegar, however, didn't begin until the fourteenth century in France. In the Middle Ages, vinegar was the great hazard of the wine trade. At first, the soured wine was considered a loss, but it didn't take long before someone turned this 'useless' liquid into a big business.

In the wine depot at Orléans, the demand for vinegar was so great that a guild of professional vinegar makers, the *Corporatif des Maîtres-Vinaigriers d'Orléans*, was established in 1394. Today, the best vinegars are still made using the old 'Orléans process'.

The process begins with the best ingredients – top-quality wine for wine vinegar and fresh, whole apples for apple cider vinegar. The liquid is placed into large wooden casks with small air holes. It is allowed to mature slowly and naturally until a film of bacteria (called the 'mother') forms on top. The 'mother' is the life force that keeps the vinegar alive and reproducing, generation after generation. At first it looks like a thick, white film. But as it matures the 'mother' grows into a gelatinous, slimy-looking thing that resembles a jellyfish.

Like good wine, the best vinegars are allowed to age properly, sometimes for several years. During the ageing process, acetic acid is formed, which gives the vinegar its tartness. (Acetic acid is simply the natural chemical that forms when wine or any other naturally fermented alcoholic beverage is allowed to sour.) The vinegar is then drawn off with a spigot at the bottom of the cask, carefully so as not to kill the 'mother'. The cask is then replenished with a fresh batch of liquid.

That is the old-fashioned method. Today, there are many vinegar producers who use modern, high-tech equipment that enables this entire process to happen in about three days. The wine (or other ingredient) is usually of poor quality; it is sprinkled with wood chips to induce a 'mother' and then heated at extremely high temperatures and aerated mechanically. While some of these 'quick' vinegars are fine for recipes that call for only a teaspoon of vinegar, they can't compare with the flavour of those vinegars that are allowed to age slowly and naturally.

When buying vinegar there is an easy way to tell which process has been used. If the vinegar has been properly aged, the label will indicate 'Made by the Orléans process', 'Aged in Wood', or *Vinaigre à l'Ancienne*. Many of the vinegar producers tell you their whole production story on the label.

In the United States, the level of acidity in vinegar must by law be printed on the label. The strength of acidity varies greatly; the higher the level, the tarter the vinegar. Generally, the highest-quality vinegars have a high acidity level of 6–7 per cent compared to conventional supermarket brands with only 4–5 per cent acidity.

VINEGAR SURVEY

Vinegar has come full circle. Centuries ago, it was considered a precious condiment fit for kings and queens. But in time, vinegar became an everyday household item and the quality suffered accordingly. Happily, vinegar's popularity and quality are on the upswing once again.

Today you can buy vinegars from around the world. The variations are endless – ranging from a sweet red rice vinegar made in China to a well-aged Italian balsamic vinegar. And, not surprisingly, the range in price is equally diverse.

What follows is a survey of the major types of vinegar, along with recommendations for those products that are superior and hints on how to use them and cook with them. In some cases, the price of the vinegar outweighs its quality, so I've given directions for making your own.

Apple Cider Vinegar

The early American colonists are said to have 'invented' apple cider vinegar by allowing the natural sugars in apple cider to ferment – first into alcohol (or what they called 'hard cider') and then into vinegar. Its most common use was for pickling vegetables, but apple cider vinegar was also used as a condiment – sprinkled into sweet soups, hearty stews, cold fruit 'salads', hot fruit compotes and over steamed fresh vegetables.

Its pungent, apple flavour was not its only appeal. For years, apple cider vinegar was used to fight the common cold, arthritis and other ailments. Some New Englanders still use it as a tonic to help aid digestion.

Today apple cider vinegar is one of the biggest-selling vinegars in the United States. Although many people consider its strong preservative powers and its inexpensive price tag to be its main attributes, a well-made apple cider vinegar can easily rival a wine vinegar. When properly aged, apple cider vinegar has a beautiful amber colour and the fresh, tart flavour of apples.

There are great differences between a fine apple cider vinegar and the odourless, tasteless stuff you find on many supermarket shelves. To begin with, a good producer will start with a wide variety of whole apples; the more types of apples that go into the vinegar, the fuller the final flavour. (Most of the cheaper brands are made from apple cores and peelings.) The apples are first ground into a sauce and then cold-pressed to extract cider. The fresh cider is placed in wooden casks where the natural sugars ferment into alcohol, or hard cider. The hard cider is transferred to other wooden casks where it is exposed to air and gradually turns to vinegar. It is allowed to age in the casks until the vinegar has mellowed and developed a full, rich flavour.

Most of the cheaper, harsher-tasting brands are artificially infused with oxygen and then bottled without being aged. Read the label to make sure you have bought a quality vinegar; it should indicate 'Made from Whole Apples Exclusively', and 'Aged in Wood'. You also want to look for a vinegar that is full-strength – 5–5½ per cent acidity. Some of the best apple cider vinegars can be found in natural food shops. Also, many apple orchards use left-over apples (and apple cider) to make vinegar. Check with your local orchard to see if they sell cider vinegar.

TASTING NOTES:

- Apple cider vinegar is delicious in salads – particularly potato salad and coleslaw.
- Add apple cider vinegar to a pumpkin soup or a rich vegetable stew. It wakes up the natural flavours of the vegetables and adds a great pungent flavour.
- Use cider vinegar as a base for home-made herb- and fruit-flavoured vinegars; see page 41 for the recipe.
- Add to home-made pickles and chutneys; see chapters 7 and 8 for recipes.
- Try making your own apple cider vinegar. It's surprisingly easy; the recipe is on page 43.

Balsamic Vinegar

Aceto balsamico is to vinegar what the Ferrari or Maserati is to cars. *Aceto* the Italian word for vinegar, and *balsamico*, which loosely translated means 'that which is good for your health,' is unlike any other type of vinegar. It has been made in and around the city of Modena, in the Emilia-Romagna region, for at least a millennium. Accordingly to Waverley Root, in his book *The Food of Italy*, 'The earliest reference to [*aceto balsamico*] dates from 1046, when Bonifacio di Canossa presented a barrel of it to Emperor Henry III as a coronation gift.'

Aceto balsamico is a rich, dark-brown vinegar that is so intensely aromatic and naturally sweet that it is sometimes used alone as a salad dressing or splashed over fresh strawberries. It has a sweet-and-sour flavour that is so refined you can drink it straight from the bottle.

Aceto balsamico is made exclusively from the must of wine grapes that contain a high sugar content, like Lambrusco, Salamino and white Trebbiano. The newly pressed must is filtered through cloth and then reduced by cooking it slowly in copper cauldrons. After the must is cooled, it is transferred to large barrels made of various specific woods. (By Italian law, the casks can be made only of oak, chestnut, mulberry or juniper.) Once in the barrels, the must is exposed to air and the sugars ferment into alcohol and finally into vinegar. The vinegar is then transferred, about once a year, to barrels made of different types of wood. To be called *aceto balsamico*, Italian law says that the vinegar must age a minimum of three years, but most of the old Modenese family vinegars are aged for closer to 50 or 100 years.

Ever since it was first made, the Italians have considered balsamic vinegar a precious commodity. In *The Food of Italy*, Root writes: 'In 1944, when the frantically clanging bells of the Ghirlandina warned Modena that American bombers were approaching, thousands took to bicycles and pedalled desperately out of the city. Many of them had time to scoop up money, jewels and other easy-to-carry valuables; and on dozens of luggage carriers small kegs were strapped. They contained vinegar.'

According to Burton Anderson, a noted expert on Italian wines and food, 'The oldest balsamic vinegars – 50, 100, 150, even 250 to 300 years old – are among the world's most expensive food products, rivalling caviare, truffles, certain ancient wines and Cognacs in value per gram . . . the oldest and finest *aceto balsamico* is for all practical purposes priceless, not for sale . . . Consider the words of Mino Durand as printed in the Italian newspaper *Corriere della Sera:* "It costs as much as liquid gold but is even more precious and he who has it won't sell it but keeps it for himself, for his children, for his grandchildren, for a few dearest friends; one might give some to the surgeon who arises in the middle of the night to operate on one's wife . . . and who, emerging at twilight from the operating room, doesn't want money but asks only for a vial of the antique elixir."'

TASTING NOTES:

There is a kind of ritual I go through when turning friends on to balsamic vinegar for the first time. First I ask them to smell it. The aroma is rich and full, without making your glands pucker up like other vinegars do. Then I pour a little of the vinegar into a spoon. As soon as they taste it, people go wild. (It's amazing how many of them want another spoonful.) Try it. You'll quickly understand why balsamic vinegar costs more than other vinegars. Listed below are just a few of my favourite ways to use balsamic vinegar:

- Balsamic vinegar is stronger than most other vinegars – you only need to use a little. Because it is so full-flavoured and naturally sweet, you can use it alone on salads without oil; it's terrific for people who are counting calories.
- Fill an avocado half with some balsamic vinegar and a touch of extra virgin olive oil.
- Try grilling a slice of crusty Italian or French bread topped with balsamic vinegar, a little olive oil and chopped garlic.
- Add a teaspoon of balsamic vinegar to an oyster or clam on the half shell and place it under the grill for a few minutes until browned.
- Use balsamic vinegar to marinate meats and chicken.
- Use balsamic vinegar to deglaze pan juices from chicken, meat or fish dishes.
- Slice an assortment of fresh wild mushrooms and toss with balsamic vinegar, olive oil and a touch of walnut oil.

- Pour the vinegar over a bowl of strawberries or a fresh fruit salad.
- For centuries, Italians have been using balsamic vinegar as a refreshing drink. Pour a glass of soda or sparkling mineral water and add a tablespoon of balsamic vinegar, a touch of sugar and a thin sliver of lemon peel.

Chinese Vinegars

The Chinese are passionate about the sweet-and-sour flavour of rice vinegar, which they have been using for thousands of years. Although vinegar is used as a cooking ingredient in a wide variety of Chinese dishes, it is most frequently used as a condiment. The three major types of Chinese vinegar are red, black and white; in general, they are all sweeter and sharper than the delicate Japanese rice vinegars. They can be found in Oriental grocers and speciality food shops.

Chinese Red Vinegar
Made from red rice, this sweet vinegar is used for two reasons: to cut the richness of certain foods and to highlight the sweetness in soups, stews and seafood. One of the most extravagant uses for red vinegar is to add a tablespoon to a bowl of hot shark's fin soup – a super rich broth made with the thin strands of meat that are removed from a shark's fin. Another traditional speciality, steamed Chinese crabs, is almost always accompanied by a small dish of red vinegar; the sweetness of the vinegar enhances the crab meat beautifully. Red vinegar can also be used as a dip for oysters on the half shell, spring rolls, steamed dumplings and fried prawns. It also makes a delicious vinaigrette mixed with pure Chinese peanut oil and chopped spring onions.

Chinese Black Vinegar
This dark-brown vinegar has a rich, sweet flavour that is similar to a Spanish sherry vinegar or an Italian balsamic vinegar. Black vinegar is believed to restore strength; in southern China it is made into a tonic and served to women after childbirth.

Like Chinese red vinegar, black vinegar is used to balance excessively rich or sweet dishes. You can buy plain black vinegar or several varieties of extra-sweet, seasoned black vinegar in Oriental grocers.

34

Chinese White or Pale Amber Vinegar

As its name implies, this is a pale-coloured rice vinegar that is frequently used in sweet-and-sour dishes and as a dressing for raw vegetables. It is quite a bit sharper than Japanese rice vinegar, and should be used in moderation.

Herb- and Fruit-Flavoured Vinegars

Within the last few years, practically every food writer has proclaimed herb vinegars (such as tarragon, basil and rosemary) and fruit vinegars (such as raspberry, strawberry and cherry) to be among the 'new ingredients of the eighties'. But herb- and fruit-flavoured vinegars have been used in America and Europe for hundreds of years.

In the 1800s, raspberry vinegar mixed with soda water and a twist of lemon was one of the most popular American summertime drinks. In her 1949 book, *Herbs – Their Culture and Uses*, Rosetta E. Clarkson writes: 'Herb vinegars, which are becoming increasingly popular, can be used to flavour ice beverages and culinary dishes and revive flagging spirits. Mint vinegar not only sharpens up a fruit punch but when patted on the forehead will relieve an aching head.'

Herb- and fruit-flavoured vinegars are made by steeping fresh herbs or fruit in apple cider or wine vinegar. It is a simple and inexpensive process, particularly when the herbs or fruit come out of your own garden. So why are these products so expensive in the shops? Like flavoured mustards, they are considered a speciality food item. That means you end up paying for fancy graphics and beautiful bottles.

There are, however, some commercially made herb and fruit vinegars that are superior and well worth their price. What makes the difference in many of these vinegars is the addition of something called a herb or fruit 'extract'. According to the catalogue of Dean & Deluca, one of the finest speciality food shops in Manhattan, 'An extract is obtained when fresh fruits or herbs are mixed with vinegar, stored in a large glass container and subjected to hours of slow hydraulic compression. After the appropriate period of seasoning, they are mechanically transformed into a paste. New vinegar is added to dilute the mass, compensate for evaporation and continue the process of seasoning. When the full concentration of flavour is reached, the resulting liquid is filtered and the extract is stored for future use.' When the vinegar is ready for bottling, a small amount of extract is added for extra flavouring. Just a few drops of raspberry extract, for example, added to a raspberry-flavoured vinegar make a world of difference. Check the label to see if extract has been added; it's a pretty good sign that the vinegar is going to be very fresh-tasting.

TASTING NOTES:
Use these herb- and fruit-flavoured vinegars with salads, in sweet-and-sour soups and stews, and with mayonnaise and cold vinaigrettes. I tasted dozens of flavoured vinegars but found the majority of them to be overpriced and artificial-tasting. It makes a lot more sense to make your own flavoured vinegars (see recipes on pages 42–4).

Japanese Rice Vinegar *(Su)*

Japanese rice vinegar is a mild, slightly sweet condiment made from rice wine. It is lighter and more delicate than American and European vinegars with a low acidity of 2–4 per cent.

Rice vinegar is a key ingredient in Japanese cuisine. The Japanese have a name for dishes made with vinegar, *sunomono*, which literally translated means 'vinegared things'. These are small salads made up of fruit, vegetables and seafood tossed with a vinegar dressing.

Another popular way of using Japanese rice vinegar is as a seasoning for *sushi* rice – that sticky, sweet rice that is served with thin slices of raw fish. Rice vinegar is used with *sushi* rice because of its gentle tartness and pleasing aftertaste. But the Japanese feel it contributes more than just good taste. In *The Book of Sushi*, Kinjirō Ōmae and Yuzuru Tachibana write: 'The observant *sushi* devotee soon notices that, despite the frequency with which they come in contact with water, *sushi* shop workers have soft, smooth hands free of cracks and blemishes. The secret of this soft skin is the mild, protective acidity of [rice] vinegar, one of the most ancient of fermented products.'

TASTING NOTES:
The delicate flavour of rice vinegar goes well with all sorts of mild food. It's a terrific vinegar to cook with – especially with chicken, fish and vegetables. Mixed with grated ginger and soy sauce, rice vinegar makes a wonderful dipping sauce. It also goes nicely with avocado and crab-meat salad.

Japanese Flavoured Vinegars

There are also an endless number of Japanese flavoured vinegars. Some of the most common include:

Aji Pon – This delicious rice vinegar is flavoured with citrus juice and soy sauce. It tastes more like a seasoned soy sauce than a vinegar; whatever it is, it's fantastic. Use in marinades, with grilled meats and fish, and as a dipping sauce for *sushi* and *sashimi*.

Sushi-Su Vinegar – This sweetened rice vinegar is used to season *sushi* rice. Sushi-Su vinegar is flavoured with sugar, corn syrup, salt and MSG. Because of the addition of MSG in most commercial brands, many Japanese cooks prefer to mix their own *sushi* vinegar at home.

Tosazu Vinegar – Another sweet vinegar, this one is flavoured with bonito (fish) stock, sugar and soy. It has a slightly fishy flavour and is used primarily for *sunomono* and as a condiment sprinkled over fish, vegetable and seaweed dishes.

Ume-Su – This vinegar is made from Japanese plums (*ume*) that are pickled with red *shiso* (beefsteak plant) leaves. It has a beautiful plum colour and a slightly salty taste. Use with vegetables, tofu and salads.

Malt Vinegar

I realised I liked malt vinegar when I first ate fish 'n' chips in England. I remember placing my order and, seconds later, being handed a newspaper cone filled with a steaming-hot assortment of fried fish and potatoes. Just as I was about to take the first bite, the lady behind the counter exclaimed, in a thick cockney accent, 'Come on, love. You ain't really expecting to eat it without the vinegar now, is you?' She then handed me a bottle of dark-brown liquid. What I remember most about that meal was not the crunchy, delicious flavour of the fried fish and potatoes but the pungent, biting taste of that malt vinegar.

Malt vinegar is made from barley that is mashed, heated with water and then fermented into a crude type of beer, known as 'gyle'. The 'beer' is placed into large vats filled with beech shavings and left to ferment for several weeks, until it turns to vinegar. Then it's filtered and coloured with caramel. The varying shades of brown you find in malt vinegars are simply the result of how much caramel has been added.

Malt vinegar has been popular in England since the early six-

37

teenth century. For some reason, it has never really caught on in the United States. A few years ago, William Woys Weaver of Paoli, Pennsylvania, wrote a letter to the *Petits Propos Culinaires*, a culinary journal, on the subject: 'Among the wealthy merchant families of Philadelphia, malt vinegar was widely used in the eighteenth and early nineteenth centuries when English tastes and customs were still in vogue here . . . Some people here felt that malt vinegar gave pickles a more characteristic flavour, but even so it had always been considered an English thing.'

TASTING NOTES:
- Serve malt vinegar with fish 'n' chips and fried chicken; it seems to cut through the greasiness of fried foods.
- Sprinkle malt vinegar over a potato salad or a cold lamb salad.
- Malt vinegar adds a delicious flavour to home-made pickles, particularly pickled onions; see recipe on page 136.
- Malt vinegar is the vinegar most often used for making pickled walnuts – a delicious condiment that is a British favourite with roast beef. See page 126 for more information about pickled walnuts.
- Add malt vinegar to barbecue sauces and marinades.

Wine Vinegars

Of all the varieties of vinegar sold today, wine vinegars are the most versatile. (For an explanation of how wine vinegar is made, see page 42.)

Wine vinegar breaks down into three major categories: those vinegars made from red and white wine; vinegar made from Spanish sherry; and champagne vinegar made from wine produced in France's Champagne region.

Red and White Wine Vinegar
Wine vinegars vary in price tremendously from the weak, 'quick method' supermarket brands to the well-aged, 'Orléans in style' vinegar. There is a big difference. A well-made vinegar can transform an ordinary salad into something incredibly good and a poor-quality vinegar can ruin any salad. I keep a fairly inexpensive French wine vinegar for everyday use and have a more expensive vinegar on hand for special meals.

Although some people like to store wine vinegar in the refrigerator, it is not necessary. However, vinegars should be kept in a cool, dark place.

TASTING NOTES:

- Wine vinegar goes particularly well in salads. Mix it into a green salad, a steamed vegetable salad or home-made coleslaw.
- Add a tablespoon or two of wine vinegar to a chicken salad, cold meat salad, prawn salad or a scallop and orange salad.
- Rub wine vinegar on roasts before cooking; it's particularly good with a leg of lamb.
- Add a dash of red wine vinegar to a cold gazpacho or hot vegetable stew.
- Add wine vinegar and chopped shallots to the frying pan when sautéing liver, chicken or beef.
- Mix wine vinegar with chopped shallots and use as a dipping sauce for clams and oysters on the half shell.
- Make a marinade with wine vinegar, olive oil, white wine, peppercorns, bay leaves and fresh herbs and use for fish fillets or a whole fish. Leave the fish to marinate for several hours and grill.

Sherry Vinegar

Sherry vinegar is made in the south-western area of Spain around Jerez. The best sherry vinegars are aged for twenty to thirty years before being bottled.

TASTING NOTES:

- Serve this rich, intensely flavoured vinegar with steamed artichokes.
- Add sherry vinegar to seafood and vegetable salads.
- Serve sherry vinegar as a dip for raw fennel.
- Use sherry vinegar to deglaze meat and poultry dishes.
- Make a vinaigrette with sherry vinegar, olive oil, capers and chopped pickles. Serve with cold prawns or shrimps, sautéed fish fillets and over cold artichoke hearts.
- Marinate spring lamb in sherry vinegar along with a few slivers of garlic. Roast, adding additional vinegar every 30 minutes, to make a pungent, sherry-flavoured glaze.
- Use sherry vinegar as a base for potato salad with bits of chopped pear.

Champagne Wine Vinegar

When you open a bottle of this (rather overpriced) vinegar, don't expect to hear the cork pop. There aren't any bubbles inside. In fact, there isn't even any Champagne.

Champagne vinegar is made from dry still white wine produced in the Champagne region of France. That's disappointing, isn't it? Well, it's not all that bad. The fact of the matter is that many champagne wine vinegars are terrific; the dry white wine produced in that part of the world is ideal for making vinegar.

TASTING NOTES:

Use champagne wine vinegar as you would any other wine vinegar – in salads, marinades and in soups. It is also a very good cooking vinegar, particularly with chicken.

MAKING YOUR OWN VINEGAR

More and more people are making their own vinegar. It's easy to do but takes some time and patience.

You should start with a bottle of left-over wine that is free of preservatives; don't use a fortified wine or a wine that has already soured. Simply cover the top of the bottle with a piece of cheese-cloth and leave it in a cool, dark spot for about four months. When you can see a 'mother' forming, you'll know the wine is being transformed into vinegar. (See page 43 for an explanation of the 'mother' and a description of how wine vinegar is made.) Once the wine has fermented, you can start using the vinegar. Each time you use some of the vinegar, remember to replenish it with additional wine.

MAKING YOUR OWN
FLAVOURED VINEGAR

The beauty of making your own flavoured vinegar at home is that you can experiment and create your own combinations. You can use any mixture of fresh herbs, fresh fruit, spices, garlic, shallots, and fruit and herb extracts (extracts are available at health food shops). (See the list of possible combinations on pages 43–4.)

Master Recipe for Home-made Flavoured Vinegar

Making flavoured vinegar is extremely easy. The only requirement is that the herbs or fruit you use be *very fresh*. These vinegars make wonderful gifts – make them in the summer when everything is ripe and fresh and then give them as Christmas gifts. The basic 'recipe' is as follows:

1. Choose an attractive bottle. It can be an old wine, Champagne, or beer bottle. Wash and rinse in boiling water and dry thoroughly.
2. In a stainless steel saucepan, heat enough apple cider, red, white or sherry wine vinegar to fill the bottle. Heat it over a low heat without letting it boil; you simply want to warm it up.
3. When making a herb-flavoured vinegar, use about 4 tablespoons of fresh herbs to 450 ml/¾ pint of vinegar – it really depends on the strength of the herbs you choose. (The herbs can be on or off the stem.) For fruit-flavoured vinegars, use about 175 g/6 oz of fresh fruit to 250 ml/8 fl oz of vinegar. Clean the herbs or fruit, and place in the bottle. Cover with the warm vinegar and allow to cool before sealing.
4. Place the vinegar in a cool, dark spot for about 10 days to two weeks before tasting. Once you can really taste the herb or fruit flavour then the vinegar is ready; if the vinegar is still weak, let it stand for another few days.
5. At this point, you can either leave the herbs and fruit in the bottle or strain the vinegar through a piece of cheesecloth and discard the herbs or fruit. Then put the vinegar back in the bottle.

Strawberry and Pepper Champagne Wine Vinegar

Strawberries and Champagne are such a natural match that I decided to try them together in a vinegar. The ripe strawberries and the peppercorns permeate the champagne wine vinegar and leave a fresh strawberry flavour, with just a subtle hint of pepper. The strawberry-coloured vinegar that results is exquisite. Use this vinegar with green salads, fruit salads, served over grilled chicken and on mild types of fish, such as fillet of sole.

175 g/6 oz ripe strawberries, thinly sliced
6 whole, black peppercorns
250 ml/8 fl oz champagne wine vinegar, or a good
dry white wine vinegar

Place the berries and peppercorns into a clear bottle or preserving jar and cover with the vinegar. Seal the jar tightly and allow to stand for about two weeks. The vinegar should turn a reddish-pink colour and have the taste and smell of fresh strawberries. Strain the vinegar through a piece of cheesecloth and discard the strawberries. Pour the vinegar into a clean bottle or jar and seal. Use within two months. *Makes about 250 ml/8 fl oz.*

Bill Bell's Red and Green Chilli Pepper Vinegar

This recipe was given to me by Bill Bell, a good friend from Portsmouth, New Hampshire. Long, thin red and green chilli peppers are stuffed into a clean wine bottle and then covered with a good apple cider vinegar; the result is a wonderful-tasting and beautiful-looking vinegar.

This vinegar is delicious sprinkled over salads, fried eggs, and in potato salad. As you use the vinegar, you should replenish it with additional apple cider vinegar.

about 750 g/1½ lb red and green chilli peppers
whole-apple cider vinegar

Wash the peppers and allow to dry. Fill a clean, clear wine bottle with the peppers until they come to the top of the bottle. Fill the bottle with the vinegar and cork. Allow to stand for 24 hours before using. *Makes about 175 ml/6 fl oz.*

Home-made Apple Cider Vinegar

Making your own apple cider vinegar is incredibly easy. Start with a good, pure apple cider; that means no preservatives or additives. Simply strain the cider through a triple layer of cheesecloth or a clean tea towel (in order to remove any sediment) into a large crock or dark-coloured glass bottle. (You can also use a plain glass jar and wrap it in foil to keep out the light.) Fill the bottle about three-quarters full and cover with a triple layer of cheesecloth; this allows the air to get in, but keeps out dust and insects.

Let the cider ferment in a cool, dark spot for about four months. (If you feel impatient and want more immediate results, add about 120 ml/4 fl oz good apple cider vinegar or dry white wine to speed up the fermentation process.) After three to four months, check the vinegar. It should be a clear, cider colour and a large, gelatinous 'mother' floating on the top. If it tastes strong and vinegary, it's ready to use; if it still tastes weak, leave for another few weeks. Carefully strain the vinegar through a triple layer of cheesecloth and pour into clean bottles. If you feel that the vinegar is too strong, simply dilute it with a bit of water. Add a fresh batch of cider to the 'mother' and repeat.

Ginger-Apple Vinegar

Slivers of fresh ginger give apple cider vinegar a refreshing (and slightly peppery) flavour. Use with steamed fish, on salads and with stir-fried vegetables.

7.5 cm/3 in piece of fresh ginger
250 ml/8 fl oz whole apple cider vinegar
1 teaspoon sugar

Peel the ginger and slice into five thin pieces. Using a sharp knife, score an X into each piece. Place the ginger in a small, clear jar and add the vinegar and sugar. Cover the jar and leave for 10 days. Strain the vinegar and discard the ginger. Clean out the jar and add the vinegar. Use sparingly. *Makes 250 ml/8 fl oz.*

Favourite Flavoured Vinegar Combinations

- White wine vinegar with rosemary and orange rind
- White wine vinegar with tarragon and lemon balm

- Red wine vinegar with basil and garlic
- White wine vinegar with crushed dill, celery, coriander, cumin and caraway seeds
- Apple cider vinegar with mint and a touch of sugar
- Apple cider vinegar with fresh dill and dill seed
- White wine vinegar with orange slices and orange extract
- White wine vinegar with fresh raspberries
- Red wine vinegar with fresh blueberries
- Japanese rice wine vinegar with ginger
- Cider vinegar with chilli peppers and garlic
- Lemon-flavoured white wine vinegar with garlic, shallots and orange rind
- Champagne vinegar with raspberry extract and fresh raspberries

COOKING WITH VINEGAR

Japanese-Style Marinated Mushrooms

25 g/1 oz thinly sliced spring onions
1 small sweet red pepper, finely chopped
1 small green hot chilli pepper, finely chopped
120 ml/4 fl oz *mirin* (sweet Japanese rice wine)
120 ml/4 fl oz Japanese or light soy sauce
120 ml/4 fl oz olive oil
4 tablespoons minced fresh ginger
3 tablespoons Italian balsamic vinegar
2 tablespoons Japanese rice wine vinegar
1½ tablespoons sesame oil
¼ teaspoon freshly ground pepper
750 g/1½ lb small mushrooms, cleaned with stems intact

Mix all the ingredients except the mushrooms and taste for seasoning. If the marinade tastes too oily, add additional rice wine vinegar; if it's too tart and vinegary, add additional oil and soy sauce. Mix in the mushrooms and leave to marinate for at least 1 hour. Serve at room temperature or cold. *Serves 4–6.*

Chicken with Garlic in a Vinegar Sauce

This is a simple dish that can be made in under an hour. You can use any type of vinegar you want with this recipe – raspberry, red wine or sherry vinegar works particularly well. The vinegar adds a terrific, pungent flavour to the chicken and the 20 cloves of garlic add a surprisingly subtle flavour.

15 g/½ oz butter
1 tablespoon virgin olive oil
1.5 kg/3 lb chicken, cut into serving pieces
1½ teaspoons dried tarragon, or 1 teaspoon fresh
salt and freshly ground black pepper
20 whole cloves garlic, peeled
250 g/9 oz sliced mushrooms
175 ml/6 fl oz vinegar, see note above
350 ml/12 fl oz chicken stock, preferably home-made

In a large frying pan or a casserole, melt the butter with the olive oil over a high heat until hot. Brown the chicken on both sides and sprinkle with the tarragon and salt and pepper to taste. Remove the chicken to a plate. Add the garlic and mushrooms to the hot pan and sauté for about 2 minutes, or until lightly browned. Add the vinegar and boil for about 2 minutes. Add the chicken stock and bring the sauce to the boil.

Place the chicken back in the pan, reduce the heat to moderately high, and let the chicken simmer, covered, for about 40 minutes, or until cooked. (To test the chicken, place a fork or sharp knife into the skin; the juices should be yellow and not pink.) Place the chicken on a serving dish and cover with the sauce. Serve with rice. *Serves 4.*

Strawberries, Oranges and Black Olives in a Balsamic Vinegar Dressing

The idea for this refreshing salad came from Ernie Brown Goldman, an actress who lives in San Francisco. This unlikely combination is delicious; if you like, you can add walnut halves instead of black olives.

175 g/6 oz ripe strawberries, thinly sliced
3 tablespoons balsamic vinegar

1 teaspoon sugar
2 oranges, peeled and thinly sliced
65 g/2½ oz black Italian or Greek olives (or walnut halves)

Place the strawberries in a bowl with the vinegar and sugar and marinate at room temperature for about 30 minutes.

Arrange the orange slices on a serving dish and spoon the berries, without the vinegar, on top. Scatter the olives (or walnuts) on top and then pour the vinegar over the salad. Serve cold. *Serves 2.*

Bean-Sprout, Avocado, Water Chestnut and Walnut Salad with Chinese Red Vinegar Dressing

1 clove garlic, minced
1 tablespoon minced ginger
3 tablespoons Chinese red rice vinegar
5 tablespoons flavoured grapeseed oil or peanut oil
salt and pepper to taste
65 g/2½ oz assorted bean-sprouts
6 fresh water chestnuts, peeled and thinly sliced
1 avocado, thinly sliced
40 g/1½ oz walnut halves
½ small red onion, thinly sliced

In a salad bowl, mix the garlic and ginger. Whisk in the vinegar, oil, salt and pepper. Add the bean-sprouts to the middle of the bowl and arrange the water chestnuts, avocado slices, walnuts and onions around them. Serve immediately. *Serves 2–4.*

Sweet-and-Sour Red Cabbage Soup

Balsamic vinegar is what gives this delicious soup its pungent flavour. It was created by Sara Moulton, *chef tournant* at La Tulipe restaurant in New York City. The soup may be served hot or cold, but if served cold the bacon should be discarded after the fat is rendered. (This recipe first appeared in *The Cook's Magazine*.)

4 rashers bacon, diced
4 medium leeks, finely diced
1½ teaspoons allspice
½ teaspoon ground cloves
2½ teaspoons minced garlic
4 packed tablespoons brown sugar
120 ml/4 fl oz balsamic vinegar
1 small red cabbage, shredded
2 400 g/14 oz cans Italian plum tomatoes, finely chopped (with juice)
1.2 litres/2 pints chicken stock, preferably home-made
salt and freshly ground black pepper to taste

THE GARNISH
250 ml/8 fl oz soured cream
freshly chopped dill or chives

In a stainless steel pan, sauté the bacon until all the fat is rendered and the bacon is crisp, about 10 minutes. Add the leeks and cook over a low heat, covered, for about 15 minutes, or until soft. Stir in the allspice, cloves and garlic and cook for 2 minutes. Add the brown sugar and vinegar and stir until the sugar is dissolved, about 3–4 minutes. Add the cabbage and tomatoes and cook, covered, over a low heat for 30 minutes, stirring occasionally.
Add the chicken stock and bring the soup to the boil. Simmer, uncovered, for 30 minutes. Add salt and pepper to taste and serve with soured cream and chopped dill or chives on top. *Serves 6.*

Avocado with Japanese Rice Vinegar and Sesame Seeds

The mild, creamy flavour of avocado lends itself to the subtle sweetness of rice vinegar. This makes a delicious appetizer or a salad served with grilled fish.

2 tablespoons Japanese rice vinegar
½ teaspoon Japanese or light soy sauce
½ teaspoon lemon juice
½ teaspoon sesame seeds
1 ripe avocado, thinly sliced
½ teaspoon bonito (dried fish) flakes (optional)

In a small bowl, mix the vinegar, soy sauce, lemon juice and sesame seeds. Arrange the avocado slices on a serving plate, overlapping them slightly. Spoon the sauce over the avocado and sprinkle with bonito flakes, if desired. *Serves 1–2.*

Oriental-Style Beef with Two Vinegars and Sesame Oil Marinade

450 g/1 lb lean flank steak
1½ tablespoons sherry wine vinegar
1½ tablespoons red wine vinegar
3 tablespoons soy sauce
1 tablespoon cornflour (optional)
1 tablespoon tahini (ground sesame paste)
2 tablespoons minced garlic
2 tablespoons minced fresh ginger
1 small onion, thinly sliced
2 tablespoons sesame oil
2 tablespoons peanut or vegetable oil
4 spring onions, cut into 6 cm/2½ in pieces

Place the meat in the freezer for 15 minutes; remove and slice on the diagonal as thinly as possible. In a large bowl, whisk together the sherry and red wine vinegars, soy sauce, cornflour, tahini, 1 tablespoon of the garlic, 1 tablespoon of the ginger, the onion and 1 tablespoon of the sesame oil. Add the meat and marinate, uncovered, for 2–4 hours at room temperature.

In a wok or large frying pan, heat the peanut or vegetable oil over a high heat until hot. Add the remaining tablespoon of sesame oil and the remaining tablespoon of ginger and garlic. Cook for about 5 seconds, and then add the meat slices with the marinade. Add the spring onions and stir quickly; cook for about 4–5 minutes or until the meat is tender. If the mixture begins to dry out, add additional soy sauce. Serve hot with steamed rice and orange slices. *Serves 2.*

Coleslaw with Walnuts and Raisins

Vinegar and cabbage work together beautifully. This coleslaw is full of good flavours and textures, but it is the addition of vinegar that makes it really delicious.

450 g/1 lb grated red and white cabbage
65 g/2½ oz chopped walnut halves
75 g/3 oz raisins
1½ tablespoons grainy or Dijon mustard
120 ml/4 fl oz red wine vinegar
2 tablespoons balsamic vinegar (optional)
2 tablespoons olive oil
175–250 ml/6–8 fl oz mayonnaise, preferably home-made (see page 97)
4 tablespoons milk
salt and freshly ground black pepper to taste

Place the cabbage, walnuts and raisins in a large salad bowl and toss. Mix in the mustard and then the vinegar(s), oil, 175 ml/6 fl oz of the mayonnaise and the milk. Add salt and pepper to taste. If you like your coleslaw creamier, add the additional mayonnaise. Serve at room temperature or chilled. *Serves about 6.*

3

Oil

OIL IS A lot like wine. If it is well made, it will have the true taste and aroma of the raw ingredients that went into it. If it is poorly made, it can be bitter and harsh or simply bland and tasteless.

To many people, oil is just a utilitarian product used for cooking food and greasing pans. Most of the oils sold in the United States are so highly refined and deodorized that they aren't capable of doing much more. But there are also pure, unrefined oils – oils that have colour, fragrance and a luscious, sensual taste.

Consider the rich aroma and nutty flavour of hazelnuts, almonds and walnuts; the luscious, fruity taste of the olive; the light, pure, nutty essence of peanuts; and the flavour of lightly toasted sesame seeds. These are characteristics of pure, unrefined oils that complement and enhance food. They are oils that deserve to be called condiments and are best appreciated at room temperature, straight from the bottle – sprinkled over salads, vegetables, fish and meat. Of course, you can also cook with these oils but, in many cases, their distinctive flavour is lost when heated.

OIL SURVEY

Pure oils should have a good colour, a distinctive fragrance and fresh taste.

Listed below are descriptions of the major varieties of oils that can be used as condiments, with some ideas of how to use them. There's also a section on flavoured oils that will tell you which ones are worth the price and how to make your own at home.

51

Olive Oil

I have a friend in New York who spends $25 for a bottle of Italian extra virgin olive oil every few months. She isn't particularly wealthy. She isn't even an outstanding cook. But she loves olive oil and appreciates the difference between a cheap olive oil and a more expensive, first pressing, extra virgin. Some might say she's a fanatic. I think she's wise. A really good olive oil is capable of transforming everyday food into an extraordinary taste experience.

Choosing a good olive oil has become complicated. And when you're spending so much on a bottle of oil, you want to make sure you're getting something special. One way to protect your investment is by reading and understanding the label.

The first thing you'll notice is the grading: 'Virgin', 'Extra Virgin', 'First Pressing', 'Cold Pressing', etc. Don't panic. It's not nearly as complicated as it sounds.

Olives are pressed for oil three times. The first pressing is called *Extra Virgin*. It is the purest oil and the most expensive.

Extra virgin oil is made from the choicest olives. The fruit is handpicked and the oil is extracted manually by cold stone presses. (No heat is used when making extra virgin olive oil; although a hot press can extract additional oil from the olive, this oil is of poorer quality.) The sediment is then filtered out of most oils; some producers, however, believe that the sediment contains a rich, olive flavour that should be left in. (If you notice that your oil is cloudy with bits of sediment floating around the bottom of the bottle, there's no cause for alarm. It's further evidence that you've got the real thing.) Extra virgin olive oil is prized for its low acidity; to be labelled 'extra virgin', the oil can have no more than 1 per cent acid.

The second pressing of the olives is done with high pressure and with the addition of heat. These oils are labelled *Virgin Olive Oil*, *Superfine Olive Oil* and *Fine Olive Oil*. All these names refer to the same grade of oil. These oils have a higher degree of acidity, about 1.5–5 per cent.

The third pressing of oil is called *Pure Olive Oil*. Made from second and third 'hot pressings' this is the least expensive type of olive oil you can buy. Pure olive oil is usually made from lower quality olives or the pulp left over from the first two pressings. It is generally mixed with a higher grade olive oil to give it a better flavour. The word 'Pure' on the label simply refers to the fact that no other types of oil have been added.

TASTING NOTES:

The four major olive-oil-producing countries are Italy, France,

Greece and Spain. *Italian olive oil* is considered by many people to be the finest in the world – particularly those oils produced in the Tuscany, Liguria and Umbria regions. These oils are very rich (some say heavy) with a full olive flavour and a deep, almost emerald-green colour. *French olive oil* is more delicate. It's known for its sweet, fruity flavour and a light, golden-yellow colour. Many people feel that the olives grown in Provence, in south-eastern France, make the most delicate and fruity oil in the world. *Spanish olive oil* has a strong, assertive olive flavour with a thick consistency. *Greek olive oil* is also thick but has a lighter olive flavour. The Spanish and Greek oils are generally less expensive than the Italian and French.

In the last few years, there have been a growing number of *American olive oils*, produced primarily in California. In general, these oils are excellent. They range from rich, olivey, Italian-style oils to more delicate French-style oils. Since most of these oils are produced on a small scale, the prices tend to be high.

Each type of olive oil has its own purpose. Just because extra virgin oil is considered the best doesn't mean it's right for every dish.

Extra virgin olive oils should be treated with respect. You're wasting your money if you use them in complex sauces and recipes that call for dozens of ingredients. They are best served at room temperature because high heat can destroy their delicate flavour.

These are just a few of my favourite ways to use olive oil:

- There is nothing better than an extra virgin olive oil mixed with a well-aged wine vinegar sprinkled over a salad – be it made of assorted lettuce, cold seafood, lightly steamed vegetables, chicken or meat.
- Use extra virgin olive oil for making pesto sauce.
- Home-made mayonnaise and flavoured mayonnaise are particularly rich and flavourful when made with olive oil; see recipes on pages 97–9.
- Make a dipping sauce with extra virgin olive oil flavoured with equal parts coarse sea salt and coarsely chopped black pepper and serve with raw fennel and other raw vegetables.
- Spoon a tablespoon of olive oil onto a thick chunk of Italian bread and top with paper-thin slices of prosciutto and a few grindings of black pepper.
- Use virgin and pure oils for making sauces, stews, sautéed vegetables, stir-fries, roasts and pasta sauces.
- Heat 2 tablespoons of virgin olive oil over a high heat. Add sliced wild mushrooms or thinly sliced courgettes and sauté for a few minutes. Add 2 cloves of chopped garlic and some

chopped fresh herbs and sauté for another minute or two, until the vegetables begin to turn golden-brown and tender. Serve immediately.

- Heat 2½ tablespoons of virgin olive oil over a high heat. Add a tin of anchovies, 2 cloves of garlic, 2 tablespoons chopped parsley and 5 chopped pimentos and allow to soften and blend. Serve on top of pasta or steamed spinach.

Nut Oils

Oils extracted from nuts are fairly new in the United States but they have been popular in Europe for a long time. A lot of people consider these oils to be an unnecessary extravagance. But if you've ever tasted a salad of Italian *radicchio* lettuce sprinkled with walnut oil, or fillet of sole moistened with almond oil, then you know these oils are worth it. Granted, they are expensive, but a little bit of their rich, nutty flavour goes a long way.

Essentially, these oils are made by crushing nuts – almonds, walnuts or hazelnuts – and then heating them until they turn to a thick golden-brown paste. The paste is then subjected to hydraulic pressure to squeeze out every possible ounce of oil.

Almond Oil

TASTING NOTES:
Almond oil has a delicate, fresh almond flavour and a beautiful amber colour. It is delicious in vinaigrettes accompanied by flaked almonds. Instead of butter, try heating a few teaspoons of almond oil and pouring it over freshly steamed French beans or broccoli. Almond oil is particularly good with artichokes; melt a tablespoon of butter and add a tablespoon of almond oil and use as a dip for hot or cold artichokes.

Hazelnut Oil

Hazelnut oil is fairly new in the United States but has long been popular in France, where it is made. This oil has the delicate scent of fresh hazelnuts and a wonderful toasted hazelnut flavour.

TASTING NOTES:

Use hazelnut oil in vinaigrettes, sauces and added to home-made mayonnaise. It's delicious on grilled fish; see recipe on page 25. Try oiling a biscuit or cake tin with hazelnut oil; it will give a wonderful hazelnut flavour to whatever you are baking.

Walnut Oil

Walnut oil is made in the Périgord and Burgundy regions of France. Unlike other nut oils, walnut oil is made from nuts that are dried and then cold-pressed. The walnut, which contains 60 per cent oil, produces a light, delicate oil.

TASTING NOTES:

Walnut oil is terrific on salads, particularly when you combine it with bits of walnut. Add walnut oil to a chicken or turkey salad with some grapes and chopped walnuts. Brush a thin coating of walnut oil on grilled fish and steaks just before serving.

Sesame Oil

Take a sniff of this oil before you use it. Once you smell the rich, intense scent of toasted sesame seeds, you'll realise just how strong this oil is. A few drops of sesame oil can add an outrageously good flavour to many foods.

Sesame oil, which is extracted from sesame seeds, is a key ingredient in Oriental cuisine. It's primarily used for cooking (almost always in combination with other, milder oils), but it is also used as a condiment – to flavour simply prepared foods and cold salads.

There are various types of sesame oil. The thicker, brown oils, which are produced in Japan and China, have the fullest, richest flavour. The oils from the Middle East are lighter and far less aromatic.

Many health food shops sell their own brand of sesame oil. Some of them are good, but they are generally very light and almost too subtle. The best sesame oils can be found in Oriental supermarkets.

TASTING NOTES:

- A few drops of sesame oil is delicious with scrambled eggs; aside from adding flavour, sesame oil can be used, instead of butter, to keep the eggs from sticking to the pan – see recipe on page 63.

- Sesame oil adds great flavour to mild soups and stews. Add a few drops to each bowl just before serving.
- Chickens' livers with thinly sliced cucumbers stir-fried in sesame oil are delicious; the nutty flavour of the oil complements the flavour of the liver beautifully.
- Sesame oil mixed with a few tablespoons of peanut oil, soy sauce, grated ginger and sliced hot chilli peppers makes a great dipping sauce for seafood and chicken.
- One of my favourite ways to use sesame oil is to heat it with a touch of Chinese peanut oil and pour it over steamed or pan-fried fish just before serving. The hot oil sizzles the fish's skin and seeps through to flavour the flesh.
- Add sesame oil to a cold squid or lobster salad.
- Sauté French beans, artichoke hearts or thinly sliced cucumbers in sesame oil and garnish with chopped sweet red pepper.

Peanut (or Groundnut) Oil

First, a little-known fact. The peanut is actually not a nut, but a seed of the pea family. When pea pods form, they turn down and bury themselves in the ground, which is why peanuts are also called groundnuts.

Peanuts contain about 50 per cent oil. When they are cold-pressed, the oil that is extracted is pure and full of rich peanut flavour. Unfortunately, most American peanut oils are so refined that they have virtually no peanut taste. They make excellent cooking oils but shouldn't be relied on for adding flavour to foods. However, in parts of France and Asia, peanut oil is a pure, unrefined oil that is prized for its distinctive peanut flavour and nutty fragrance. These oils are generally more expensive than the refined American peanut oils, but they are definitely worth the extra expense.

TASTING NOTES:
- Because of its high smoking point, peanut oil is most frequently used as a frying oil. Use it to fry tempura, chicken, fish fillets or vegetables.
- Try heating a teaspoon or two of peanut oil with a touch of sesame oil and pouring it over steamed or stir-fried spinach or lettuce.

- Chinese peanut oil mixed with grated ginger, thinly sliced spring onions and coarse sea salt makes a fantastic dipping sauce for steamed or boiled chicken.
- Mix peanut oil, soy sauce, minced garlic, grated ginger and spring onions and serve as a dipping sauce for prawns or crab.
- Make a vinaigrette using peanut oil, sesame oil, grapefruit juice and wine vinegar. Toss with poached scallops and watercress and serve cold.

Flavoured Oil

Oils flavoured with fresh herbs, chilli peppers, garlic and spices are hot items in speciality food shops these days. While a number of these products are terrific, many are overpriced. You can make your own flavoured oils at home for a lot less; see pages 58–60 for recipes.

TASTING NOTES:
- Use flavoured oils in vinaigrettes along with fresh herbs.
- Pour flavoured oils on cold pasta and vegetable salads.
- Try making a marinade for beef or chicken using flavoured oils, vinegar, red wine and fresh herbs.
- Add a few tablespoons of herb-flavoured oils to a home-made mayonnaise (see pages 97–9).
- Brush these oils onto fish, chicken, steaks and shish kebab before grilling or barbecuing.
- Use flavoured grapeseed oils for cooking beef fondue.
- Use a basil- or mixed-herb-flavoured oil as the base of a pesto sauce.

MAKING YOUR OWN
FLAVOURED OIL

It makes a lot of sense to make your own flavoured oils. For one thing, it's generally much less expensive than buying the commercially produced oils; but the real fun of making them at home is that you can create your own combinations.

On the following pages, you'll find recipes for making herb-flavoured oils and hot chilli oil. I've also included a list of my favourite flavoured-oil combinations. Try them or experiment with your own recipes.

Master Recipe for Home-made Herb-Flavoured Oil

Making herb-flavoured oil is a great way to use up an abundance of herbs from a summer garden. Depending on the strength of the herbs you use, this oil should take anything from two to three weeks to make. Use flavoured oils in pesto sauces, herb-flavoured mayonnaise, salad dressing and with cold seafood and vegetables.

4 tablespoons fresh herbs, left on the stems, if desired
350 ml/12 fl oz virgin or extra virgin olive oil

Thoroughly wash and dry the herbs and stuff into a medium-size preserving jar or a clean bottle. Cover with the oil, seal tightly and leave to stand for two or three weeks in a cool, dark spot. After two weeks, taste the oil; it should have a definite herb flavour and aroma; if it is still weak, leave it for another few days. Strain the oil through a piece of cheesecloth and pour into a clean jar or bottle. Place a sprig or two of the fresh herbs in the jar or bottle before sealing. The oil can be refrigerated or left in a cool, dark spot. *Makes 350 ml/12 fl oz.*

Olive Oil Flavoured with Garlic, Pepper and Bay Leaf

Use this oil with seafood and grilled meats. Brush on seafood, steaks or lamb shish kebab before grilling. Use in soups and stews and with salads.

120 ml/4 fl oz olive oil, preferably extra virgin or virgin
2 whole cloves garlic, peeled
6 peppercorns
2 bay leaves

In a small, clean bottle or preserving jar, place the garlic, peppercorns and bay leaves and cover with oil. (The oil should come up to the top of the jar.) Leave for 24 hours before using. *Makes 120 ml/4 fl oz.*

Home-made Chinese Hot Chilli Oil

This hot, spicy chilli pepper oil is what gives Szechuan and Hunan dishes their fiery taste. There are many commercially produced chilli oils on the market, but many Chinese cooks feel they are too mild to be really effective.

Use this chilli oil as you would a hot sauce – with soups, stews, egg dishes and Chinese noodles. Remember: this is lethal stuff – use it sparingly.

250 ml/8 fl oz peanut oil
6 tablespoons small dried red chilli peppers, chopped
2–3 teaspoons cayenne pepper
1 teaspoon sesame oil (optional)

Heat the oil over a moderately high heat; do not let it boil or burn. Reduce the heat to low and add the chilli peppers. Cover and cook for about 10 minutes, or until the peppers turn black. Remove from the heat and allow to cool.

Once the oil is cool, stir in the cayenne pepper and sesame oil. Leave the oil to stand overnight and then strain through cheesecloth into a clean jar or bottle. Keep the oil refrigerated. *Makes 250 ml/8 fl oz.*

Favourite Flavoured-Oil Combinations

- Garlic, basil and crushed black peppercorn-flavoured olive oil
- Olive oil with chopped fresh fennel and fennel seeds
- Peanut oil with ginger, garlic and shallots
- Sesame oil with chilli peppers
- Fresh rosemary, thyme and oregano-flavoured olive oil
- Olive oil with fresh coriander, Italian parsley and crushed coriander seeds
- Red and green chilli pepper-flavoured peanut oil
- Olive oil flavoured with lemon wedges and cloves

COOKING WITH OIL

Grilled Fish Fillets with Oil

This is a simple recipe for fish grilled with oil, lemon juice and pepper. You can use any type of oil you want with this recipe; nut oils – almond, hazelnut and walnut – are particularly good, but virgin olive, sesame and peanut oil are also delicious.

> 4 teaspoons oil (see note above)
> 450 g/1 lb fish fillets, such as sole or haddock
> generous grinding of black pepper
> 2 teaspoons lemon juice

Preheat the grill. Spread 2 teaspoons of the oil on to the bottom of a shallow baking dish or an ovenproof frying pan. Place the fish fillets in the dish and sprinkle generously with pepper. Add the lemon juice and remaining 2 teaspoons of oil equally over the fish and grill for 5–7 minutes, or until the fish flakes easily when tested with a fork. Serve with lemon and lime wedges. *Serves 2.*

Sun-dried Tomatoes Marinated in a Peppered Olive Oil

In Liguria, Italy, perfectly ripe plum tomatoes are dried out in the hot summer sun until they shrivel up and look like dried chilli peppers. Like any other type of dried food, the tomatoes intensify in flavour; one sun-dried tomato tastes like a dozen fresh ones. They are sold in two forms: dried, and marinated in a seasoned olive oil. Because the marinated tomatoes are so expensive, I prefer to buy the dried variety and marinate them myself. It's definitely worth a really good extra virgin olive oil with this marinade. Not only will the tomatoes soak up the olive flavour, but, when the tomatoes are gone, you'll be left with a delicious tomato-pepper-flavoured oil. Serve these tomatoes with fish, meats, chicken or in antipasto and salads. The flavoured oil is wonderful over pasta salads and for sautéing fresh vegetables.

These tomatoes make a wonderful gift. Place the tomatoes in an attractive preserving jar, cover with the olive oil and seasonings, and seal the jar tightly. Place a label on the jar explaining how the tomatoes are used and give to a good friend.

about 15 sun-dried tomatoes
1 small red chilli pepper, crumbled
2 cloves garlic
2 bay leaves
4 black peppercorns
1 tablespoon pine nuts (optional)
about 120 ml/4 fl oz extra virgin olive oil

Place the tomatoes in a bowl and cover with lukewarm water. Leave for about 15 minutes, or until soft. Drain and dry thoroughly on paper towels.

Into a small, clean preserving jar (or used spice bottle), place half the chilli pepper, 1 clove of garlic, 1 bay leaf, 2 peppercorns and ½ tablespoon of the nuts. Place half of the tomatoes on top and cover with about 4 tablespoons of the oil. Place the remaining ingredients on top and cover with the remaining oil. (The oil should come to the top of the jar; add additional oil if needed.) Leave for at least 24 hours before using.

Gingered Chicken Broth with Watercress, Spring Onions and Sesame Oil

This soothing chicken broth is spiked with the refreshing flavour of fresh ginger. A drop or two of hot sesame oil is added to each bowl of soup just before serving; it adds a wonderful nutty flavour without making the soup the least bit greasy or oily.

1 litre/1¾ pints chicken stock, preferably home-made
4 thin slices fresh peeled ginger, about 5 mm/¼ in thick
4 spring onions, cut down the middle lengthwise and cut into 5 cm/2 in pieces
1 bunch watercress
2 teaspoons Oriental sesame oil

In a medium-size saucepan, heat chicken stock with the ginger over a medium heat. Simmer, covered, for about 5 minutes.

Add the spring onions and watercress and simmer until the greens are just soft, about 1–2 minutes. Meanwhile, heat the sesame oil in a small saucepan and let it get very hot, without burning or smoking. Add a few drops of the hot oil to each bowl of soup before serving. *Serves 4.*

Fillet of Sole with Flaked Almonds Sautéed in Almond Oil

25 g/1 oz butter
2½ tablespoons almond oil
450 g/1 lb fillet of sole
25 g/1 oz flour, seasoned with salt and black pepper
50 g/2 oz flaked almonds
lemon wedges

In a large frying pan, melt the butter with 1 tablespoon of the oil over a medium-high heat. Lightly flour the sole and when the butter and oil are hot, sauté the fillets for about 2 minutes on each side. Transfer to a warm platter and cover to keep warm.

Add the remaining 1½ tablespoons of oil to the frying pan and sauté the almonds until golden brown. Spoon the almonds over the sole and serve with lemon wedges. *Serves 2.*

Chinese-Style Scrambled Eggs with Sesame Oil

This recipe was inspired by my friend Ken Hom, a renowned Chinese chef and author of *Chinese Technique* (Simon & Schuster). Hom prepares eggs scrambled with sesame oil, bean sprouts and tiny Chinese eels in a wok. The sesame oil not only flavours them but also keeps them from sticking to the wok. This is a great brunch dish or just a new way to make an everyday breakfast a little bit different. I've omitted the eels.

4 large eggs
1½ teaspoons Oriental sesame oil
15 g/½ oz bean sprouts
2 tablespoons thinly sliced spring onions
2 muffins or pieces of toast

In a bowl, beat the eggs with 1 teaspoon of the sesame oil. Heat a wok or a frying pan over a high heat until it is very hot. Add the eggs and stir quickly; sprinkle in the sprouts and spring onions and stir the eggs around until cooked, about 2–3 minutes. Serve on toasted muffins or toast and trickle with the remaining ½ teaspoon of sesame oil. *Serves 2.*

Sautéed Prawns in a Sesame Oil-Mustard-Orange-Soy Sauce

1½ tablespoons sesame oil
1 tablespoon virgin olive oil
3 cloves minced garlic
3 tablespoons minced fresh ginger
3 spring onions, sliced down the centre and cut into 4 cm/1½ in pieces
450 g/1 lb small or medium prawns, peeled
1 tablespoon Dijon or grainy mustard
120 ml/4 fl oz fresh orange juice
1½ tablespoons light Chinese or Japanese soy sauce
freshly grated pepper to taste

In a wok or a large frying pan, heat the oils over a high heat. Add the garlic and ginger and sauté for 2–3 seconds, or until lightly browned. Add the spring onions and prawns and sauté for 1 minute. Whisk in the mustard, orange juice and soy sauce and let the sauce come to the boil; reduce the heat and simmer about 4–5 minutes, or until the prawns are cooked. Remove the prawns with a slotted spoon to a warm serving platter and let the sauce boil for another minute, until slightly thickened. Pour over the prawns and season with pepper to taste. Serve with rice or buttered noodles. *Serves 2–4.*

Coffee-Almond Slices

This buttery pound cake is flavoured with almond oil and vanilla and baked in a bread tin that has been greased with almond oil. It is covered with a delicious, simple coffee-almond butter icing.

THE CAKE
2½ teaspoons almond oil
4 eggs, thoroughly beaten
175 g/6 oz caster sugar
65 g/2½ oz plain flour, sifted twice
¼ teaspoon vanilla extract

THE ICING
100 g/4 oz butter, softened
175 g/6 oz sugar
about 4 tablespoons very strong coffee

THE GARNISH
15 g/½ oz butter
1 teaspoon almond oil
50 g/2 oz flaked almonds

To make the pound cake: Preheat the oven to 180°C/350°F/Gas Mark 4. Lightly grease a bread tin with 1½ teaspoons of the almond oil and set aside. Place the eggs and sugar in a large bowl set over simmering water. Whisk vigorously until thickened, about 10–15 minutes. Remove from the heat and let the mixture cool slightly. Gently fold in the sifted flour and then mix in the remaining teaspoon of almond oil and the vanilla. Place the mixture in the greased tin and bake for 15–25 minutes, or until a toothpick inserted in the centre comes out clean. Remove the cake from the tin and place on a wire rack.

Meanwhile, *prepare the icing:* In a large bowl, cream the butter with the sugar until thoroughly blended and creamy. Mix in the coffee, a tablespoon at a time, until the icing turns a light coffee colour and has a subtle coffee taste.

Prepare the garnish: In a small frying pan, melt the butter with the almond oil over a moderately high heat. Sauté the almonds for about 3–5 minutes, or until they turn a golden brown. Remove and drain on paper towels.

When the cake is cool, spread the top and sides with the icing and scatter the sautéed almonds along the top. Cut into thin slices and serve with strong coffee laced with Amaretto.

4

Hot Pepper Sauces and Horseradishes

Salsas, Sambals, *Chinese Chilli Sauces, Tabasco,* Wasabi

THERE ARE CERTAIN chapters in this book which will always be memorable for me. Olive oil, for example, turned out to be a luscious, sensual subject to write about. The tastings for that chapter were equally pleasant – exquisite extra virgin olive oils sprinkled over bowls of fresh pasta, thick slices of ripe tomatoes and chunks of crusty French bread. This chapter, on the other hand, was a bit different. It involved tears; it involved screaming and coughing; it involved fits of complete pain. After tasting close to one hundred different hot pepper sauces from around the world, I wondered if there was a clause in my insurance policy for severe indigestion.

Hot sauces are eaten all over the world. In Japan a green horseradish root is ground into a fiery hot paste and eaten with *sushi* and *sashimi*; in Mexico, a mixture of chopped chilli peppers, tomatoes, onions, spices and lime juice is used to season everything from corn tortillas to grilled steak. Red chilli peppers ground with peanuts and tamarind juice are served with barbecued foods throughout Indonesia; and in Bermuda, chilli peppers steeped in dry sherry are a favourite island tradition. In the United States, chilli peppers, tomatoes, onions and spices are mixed to make a wide variety of sauces; and throughout China there are probably as many variations of chilli sauce as there are chefs to create them.

Most hot pepper sauces are developed in countries with a tropical climate. For years I've heard that hot sauces will actually keep you cool when the weather is hot. And doctors and scientists have proven that chilli peppers do stimulate the circulation and raise the temperture of your body. According to Jane Brody, health editor of *The New York Times*, 'If you are living in a hot climate, the increase in body temperature can make you feel cooler by diminishing the difference between you and the surrounding air by inducing sweating, which cools the body when the perspiration evaporates.'

Chilli peppers are loaded with vitamins A and C and when they're ground up into a sauce, they can clear your sinuses, ease your asthma and stimulate your appetite. But the real appeal of a hot pepper sauce is its powerful flavour. A really good hot sauce takes you by the shoulders, gives you a good shake, and slaps your face to say 'HELLO.'

However, if you've eaten a hot sauce that just happens to be a bit too hot, don't reach for a glass of water, beer, wine or tea. Liquids scatter the oils in the chilli pepper all over your tongue. What you want when the fire's too hot is to eat something that will soak up the peppery oils; try a piece of bread or a bite of noodles or rice. The most soothing thing possible after a bite of fire is to dip into a bowl of yogurt mixed with grated cucumber and chopped mint. It's like jumping into a swimming pool on a scorching day.

HOT SAUCE SURVEY

Chinese Chilli Sauces

When I was about twelve years old, I remember my parents taking me to a restaurant in New York's Chinatown. To begin we had a plate of freshly made shrimp dumplings which arrived, much to my delight, with a choice of dipping sauces – hot Chinese mustard, a flavoured soy sauce, gooey sweet duck sauce and a tiny bowl of bright-red Chinese chilli sauce. I opted for the red stuff, submerged the dumpling into the tiny bowl and then, naively, popped the entire dumpling into my mouth. The next thing I remember was a stream of tears. But as the sauce crept down my throat, and I got my breath back, I suddenly realised this was an incredible taste sensation; I was hooked.

Chinese chilli sauces can be overwhelming, but they can also be deliciously subtle. Each Chinese province is known for its own type of sauce, ranging from a simple blend of chilli peppers, garlic and vinegar to more sophisticated black bean chilli sauces. (See recipe on page 78.)

TASTING NOTES:
Chinese chilli sauces tend to be thick. They are most often served as dipping sauces for grilled meats, roast duck, chicken, spare-ribs, dumplings and savoury pastries. Used sparingly, Chinese chilli sauce can also add a wonderful peppery flavour to noodle and rice dishes and stir-fried foods.

Harissa *(Moroccan Hot Sauce)*

Harissa, made from a blend of dried red chilli peppers, salt, lemon juice and spices, is a fiery-hot Tunisian sauce. It's traditionally served with *couscous*, a fine grain (made from semolina flour) which is steamed and served with a spicy stew (usually made of lamb or chicken with large chunks of fresh vegetables). The *couscous* is served in a large bowl and the meat and vegetable stew is ladled on top. A small dab of *harissa* is mixed into the gravy to give the dish an extra peppery bolt.

TASTING NOTES:
In addition to *couscous*, *harissa* also adds delicious flavour to soups, stews, pasta sauces, goulash, rice dishes, cold meats and grilled fish. Many of the commercially made brands of *harissa* are super thick and pasty; you may want to thin them down with fresh lemon juice and olive oil. Although some of these brands of *harissa* have a good, hot bite, nothing can compare with a freshly made *harissa*; see page 79 for the recipe.

Horseradish

When I was a child, horseradish was always to be found in our refrigerator. We ate it on brisket and potato pancakes, gefilte fish and dark rye bread, roast beef and thin slices of boiled ham. But for years, I never realised that horseradish came from a root; to me it was always just that hot white stuff in a jar.

A relative of the mustard family, horseradish is the most pungent of all edible roots. It is native to Eastern Europe and Western Asia; it grows wild and is also cultivated throughout Europe, England and the United States.

No one seems to know how horseradish got its name. But Steven Gold, whose family has been making horseradish in Brooklyn, New York, since 1932, offers one possible explanation. According to Gold, horseradish comes from the German word *Meerrettich*, meaning, 'sea radish'. Horseradish, he claims, grew wild along the seashore and was also sometimes known as 'the galloping radish', which may have led to its name.

For hundreds of years, horseradish was prized as a medicinal herb. In the first century, Pliny claimed horseradish would dissolve gallstones and help cure asthma. And there are still some people who swear by it for clearing sinuses and curing a winter cold. Like hot chilli peppers, fresh horseradish is loaded with vitamin C.

It wasn't until the sixteenth century that horseradish was used for culinary purposes. In *Stalking the Healthful Herbs*, Euell Gibbons writes: 'One herbalist finally mentions its use by the Germans "as a sauce to eat fish with and such meats as we do mustarde," but it is not until 1640 that a writer mentions its use as a condiment in England, and he damns it with faint praise, writing that it is used only by "country people and strong labouring men," and adding "it is too strong for tender and gentle stomachs." Not long after, however, horseradish did begin to appear on the tables of the gentry.'

Today the biting, pungent flavour of horseradish is one of the most popular condiments in England. Roast beef served with freshly grated horseradish sauce is as commonplace as a hamburger with ketchup in the United States. Horseradish has become increasingly popular in the last few years in the United States. You now find it in elegant restaurants served with raw fish, smoked fish and meats. Horseradish is used in a wide variety of sauces and is frequently found floating in glasses of spicy Bloody Marys.

TASTING NOTES:

- Serve horseradish with roast beef, smoked ham, tongue or lamb.
- A pot of horseradish should always be on the table when serving corned beef and cabbage or boiled beef.
- Horseradish goes particularly well with fish – raw oysters and clams on the half shell, smoked fish (particularly trout), boiled prawns and crabs.
- Around the Jewish holidays horseradish can be found more easily in many grocery stores. Horseradish is one of the five symbolic foods traditionally placed on the Seder plate at Passover; it symbolises the suffering the Jews felt when they fled Egypt. Horseradish is also served with other Jewish foods – gefilte fish, boiled beef, brisket and herring.
- In France, fresh horseradish root is brought to the table and each person slices off a small piece and sprinkles it generously with coarse sea salt. It is said to stimulate the appetite.
- Horseradish mixed with grated apple and soured cream is delicious with *schnitzel*, pork chops, or thin slices of roast ham.
- Add horseradish to a Bloody Mary; it gives the drink a spicy punch and nice texture.
- Mix freshly grated horseradish into a cocktail sauce and serve with boiled prawns, raw clams or fried oysters.
- Shave thin slices off a fresh horseradish root and serve on top of a grilled steak.

- Add a teaspoon of horseradish to a spicy Dijon mustard and spread it on top of fish fillets and grill. It makes a spicy horseradish-mustard glaze.
- Mix horseradish into a home-made mayonnaise (see page 97 for the recipe) and use as the base for a turkey, egg or chicken salad.
- Try serving boiled new potatoes or steamed asparagus with a simple sauce made of melted butter, a few teaspoons of prepared horseradish and chopped fresh dill.
- Other ideas for using horseradish are on pages 85–8.

Indian Hot Sauces

In India they are called hot oil pickles, but to me they seem more like thick, chunky sauces. Ultimately, it's a matter of semantics. What counts with these condiments is their intense heat. They're made from all sorts of fruits and spices – mangoes, limes, lemons, aubergines, ginger and lotus stems – but the crucial ingredient is the chilli pepper. These Indian pickles are, above all else, tremendously hot. To place them anywhere else in this book would be inappropriate.

Indian pickles are quite different in taste and texture from Western pickles. The fruits are preserved in oil with a variety of spices and chilli peppers and they eventually 'dissolve' into a thick, fiery-hot sauce. Indian pickles must be eaten in minute quantities and always with other foods.

TASTING NOTES:
Indian pickles are traditionally eaten with curries, particularly vegetable and seafood curries. They also go well with grilled chicken, barbecued meats, and Indian breads and deep-fried savoury pastries.

Mexican *Salsas* and Other Latin American Hot Pepper Sauces

There are over one hundred varieties of chilli peppers growing throughout Latin America, so it's no wonder that they are such an important part of the diet. There is an equally astounding number of *salsas* (sauces) made from these peppers. They can be raw or cooked and range from mildly spicy to 'oh-my-God-please-help-me' hot.

71

The most familiar is the Mexican *salsa picante* (hot sauce) or *salsa cruda* (raw sauce) – both are combinations of chopped fresh tomatoes, onions, chilli peppers (usually serrano or jalapeño), lime juice (or vinegar), salt and spices. *Salsa picante* is the basis for a number of other hot sauces. The Chilean pepper sauce called *pebre* uses the same ingredients, with the addition of olive oil. Throughout Texas and New Mexico, there are now hundreds of *salsas picantes*, each with its own slight variation.

Salsa verde (green sauce) is another popular hot sauce made from *tomatillos*, Mexican green husk tomatoes. *Tomatillos* have a distinctive flavour, quite different from ordinary green tomatoes, and when they are chopped and mixed with fresh *cilantro* (coriander), chilli peppers, onions and garlic, they make a spicy and somewhat sour sauce.

Salsa ranchera (country sauce) is a simple combination of tomatoes, chilli peppers, garlic and onions cooked in oil. It is the classic accompaniment to *huevos rancheros* – a Mexican breakfast dish of fried eggs served on freshly made tortillas.

TASTING NOTES:

Mexican *salsas* and Latin American pepper sauces go best with simply cooked foods – fried eggs, grilled steak, barbecued chicken, pork and pan-fried fish. Of course, they also go well with more traditional Mexican food – tacos, tortillas, guacamole and taco chips, *burritos*, enchiladas, *quesadillas* and *tostadas*.

The traditional way to enjoy these sauces is to make up a small batch at home. Although there are now a large number of terrific *salsas* sold in ethnic and speciality food shops, the bottled sauces never seem to match the flavour and texture of a freshly made hot pepper sauce. (See recipes on pages 81–3.)

Sambals

Sambals are fiery-hot pepper sauces that are served with a wide variety of South-East Asian dishes. The word *sambal* describes a range of condiments – from an exotic mixture of chilli peppers blended with garlic, shallots, tamarind juice and shrimp paste to a peanut-butter-based sauce. A *sambal* can be raw or cooked, killer-hot or mild, but the one thing all *sambals* have in common is hot chilli peppers.

Sambals are most commonly eaten with Indonesian food. They are an important part of the traditional Indonesian banquet called *rijsttafel* ('rice table'). The banquet consists of a huge plate of boiled rice, surrounded by some twenty to thirty 'side' dishes, of which at least four or five are *sambals*. Critics often judge *rijsttafel* according to the number and quality of home-made *sambals* served.

Indonesians take their *sambals* seriously. An old Indonesian proverb declares that even an 'ugly girl' can find a husband if she can brew good coffee and make a good *sambal*.

TASTING NOTES:
There are as many uses for *sambals* as there are types. They complement mild-flavoured rice dishes, grilled beef, pork or chicken *satay*, egg rolls, noodle dishes, grilled prawns and stir-fried vegetables. Serve *sambals* as you would a hot pepper sauce or spicy relish.

Sherry Peppers Sauce

Bermuda has long been famous for its beautiful sandy beaches, idyllic scenery, and vacationing honeymooners. But one of the island's few native products has recently gained an international reputation.

Sherry peppers sauce is made by steeping hot chilli peppers and spices in casks of dry sherry. After several months, the liquid is transformed into a spicy, hot pepper sauce. Yeaton Outerbridge, a native Bermudian, has been bottling sherry peppers sauce since 1964, but the history of the sauce goes back many years. According to Outerbridge: 'Bermudians first came to know sherry peppers back in the sailing vessel days of the Royal Navy. After several months at sea, the quality of the food aboard ship attained a degree of ripeness that made a strongly flavoured seasoning a necessity. An enterprising officer ashore in Bermuda saw the small native "bird" pepper. This was a particularly "hot" pepper which the officer thought might be used to disguise the taste of the provisions aboard and make them palatable. So he took the peppers, steeped them in sherry and . . . a new condiment was born.'

TASTING NOTES:

Sherry peppers sauce can be used like any other hot pepper sauce, but the sherry gives it a unique flavour. It's particularly good in soups and fish chowders, in sauces, marinades and barbecue sauce. Sprinkle it over fried eggs, fried tomatoes and pan-fried fish. (See page 83 for a recipe for making your own home-made version of sherry peppers sauce.)

Tabasco Sauce

After tasting over a hundred different hot pepper sauces from around the world, I've come to the inevitable conclusion that Tabasco is the best. It has a perfect balance of heat and good peppery flavour – a punch, but not a knockout.

The history of Tabasco is one of those great American success stories. It begins with the McIlhenny family of Avery Island, Louisiana, a narrow, 2,500-acre stretch of land jutting above the Gulf Coast. Avery Island is not really an 'island'; it's actually an oversized hill built on top of a large salt dome. The Avery and McIlhenny families have owned the 'island' since 1818 and for years the main industry there was salt mining. But in 1848 all that changed.

A friend of Edmund McIlhenny, named Gleason, returned from the Mexican War bringing with him hot Mexican chilli peppers. Gleason raved about the peppers' spicy taste and their ability to enhance the flavours of other foods. McIlhenny decided to sow the pepper seeds at his father-in-law's plantation on Avery Island, and before long he had a field of bright-red peppers.

Then McIlhenny had an idea. He wanted to capture the spicy essence of these exotic peppers in a sauce. After many failed experiments, he developed what he called the 'perfect hot pepper sauce'. In 1868, McIlhenny filled 350 bottles with the bright-red spicy liquid and sold them to select wholesalers across the country. It was a hit. By 1870, he had received orders for over a thousand bottles. Just two years later the demand for the sauce had grown so great that McIlhenny opened a branch in London in order to accommodate the orders that were pouring in from Great Britain and Europe. Today the McIlhenny family produces

200,000 to 300,000 bottles of Tabasco sauce *a day*. Their sauce had become so famous around the world that the name Tabasco has practically become a generic term for all hot pepper sauces.

The recipe for Tabasco sauce hasn't changed much over the years. It all starts with tabasco peppers, a strain of peppers developed by McIlhenny. (The word *tabasco* is an Indian term meaning 'where the soil is humid'. And it is the heat and moisture of the Southern soil that helps the tabasco pepper develop its distinctive flavour.)

Tabasco sauce is made by a slow, precise process. In early spring the tabasco pepper seedlings are transplanted from greenhouses and hotbeds to the fields of Avery Island. In the next few months, the land is transformed into a kind of magical carpet; peppers in different stages of growth – oranges, yellows and reds – pop up from the rich earth in a wild splash of colour.

In the late summer, the ripe red peppers are harvested. They are crushed with Avery Island rock salt to create a 'mash', and then placed into white oak barrels covered with perforated lids. A layer of rock salt is spread over the top of the lid to keep air out and let gases escape. The mash is allowed to ferment and develop flavour for close to three years. It is then inspected (often by Walter McIlhenny, president of the McIlhenny Co. and grandson of its founder) for colour, aroma and flavour. The mash that passes inspection is then blended with distilled vinegar and placed into 2,000-gallon oak vats. For four weeks, the mixture is gently stirred with wooden paddles. The sauce is then strained and filtered before being placed into the traditional, narrow-necked Tabasco bottle.

TASTING NOTES:

I use Tabasco with just about everything. The little red bottle sits on the table through every meal; I just can't get enough of it.

Tabasco can be used as a table condiment or you can cook with it. You should always remember that, like garlic and onions, the longer it cooks the more its flavour is dissipated. The best way to taste the flavour of Tabasco is to add it just before serving so it has a chance to heat through and not disappear.

Here are a few of my favourite ways to use Tabasco:

- Try sprinkling a few drops on fried, scrambled or poached eggs. It's also terrific in a red-and-green-pepper omelette.
- Add Tabasco to raw clams and oysters on the half shell.
- Sprinkle a few drops into soups, stews and casseroles just before serving.
- Serve with sautéed fish, fried clams and cold boiled prawns.

- Try adding a few drops to a Bloody Mary to give it a spicy bite.
- Sprinkle a few drops of Tabasco on steaks, chicken and shish kebab just a few minutes before they finish cooking under the grill.
- Add Tabasco to pasta sauces just before you toss it with the pasta.
- Add to marinades and sauces instead of black pepper or peppercorns.
- I have a friend who swears Tabasco adds an amazing flavour to apple and pumpkin pies; try it.
- Sprinkle Tabasco, instead of ketchup, on chips and hamburgers.
- Add a few drops of Tabasco sauce to a home-made (or even a bottled) barbecue sauce to give it an extra bite.

Thai Hot Chilli Sauce *(Nam Prik)*

Some time ago, while I was sitting in Bangkok Cuisine, my favourite Thai restaurant in Boston, I overheard the following conversation: 'Well, what do you think? Isn't Thai food fantastic?' a young male student asked his female companion. 'It's okay,' she replied, 'but the condiments are outrageous.' She was referring to the platter of pungent Thai fish sauce, chopped peanuts, pickled chilli peppers, flakes of dried red chilli peppers, and fiery-hot pepper sauce that is served with every meal.

Thai hot sauce or *Nam Prik*, is found on tables throughout Thailand. According to Jennifer Brennan, author of *The Original Thai Cookbook*, '*Nam Prik* sauce is the universal favourite of the Thai people through all strata of society. It is one of the ancient, traditional dishes of the country, records indicating that it was probably eaten in the twelfth and thirteenth centuries during the Sukhothai period. . . .'

Brennan goes on to say that 'every meal will be accompanied by at least one or two sauces and they play as important a part within their cuisine as the French sauces do within their cuisine.' Essentially, *Nam Prik* is made from ground chillies, vinegar, salt and sugar. Other common ingredients include peanuts, garlic, shallots, coconut cream, fish sauce, dried shrimp, shrimp paste, raw aubergine, and tamarind liquid. *Nam Prik* is generally thick and gooey like ketchup. (See recipe for making your own on page 78.)

Saus Prik is a sweeter version of *Nam Prik*. Made with the addition of sugar, raisins, tomatoes and sweet jam, it's particularly popular with seafood and spring rolls.

76

Thai hot sauces go well with all sorts of Oriental cuisine – curries, light soups, rice dishes, grilled meats and noodles. *Pad Thai*, a Thai fried noodle dish with prawns, bean-sprouts, fresh coriander and ground peanuts is superb topped with a teaspoon of Thai hot sauce. These sauces are also good mixed in a chicken or cold beef salad, or served with fried chicken, barbecued pork or spareribs and with fried or scrambled eggs.

Wasabi (Japanese Green Horseradish)

Wasabi, the Japanese word for 'mountain hollyhock', is a green horseradish root that grows wild throughout Japan on flooded mountain terraces and at the edge of cold, clear streams. Fresh *wasabi* root is difficult to buy elsewhere. However, dry powdered *wasabi* can be found in Oriental and speciality food shops.

Wasabi is more fragrant and sharp than white horseradish. A teaspoon of ground *wasabi* has a potent, powerful bite that will clear your sinuses within seconds. Like other hot, peppery foods, *wasabi* stimulates the appetite and is rich in vitamin C.

TASTING NOTES:
Wasabi is sold in powdered or paste form. The powdered *wasabi* is preferable because it never goes bad and you can mix it up as you need it.

Similar to powdered mustard; simply add a small amount of tepid water to the *wasabi* powder and mix until it forms a smooth, thick paste. Allow the paste to stand for about 10 minutes to develop full flavour.

The most popular use for *wasabi* is mixed into soy sauce to make a dipping sauce for *sushi* and *sashimi*. In addition, *wasabi* is dabbed onto the rice in *sushi* rolls to give the raw fish a fresh, cleansing flavour. (It is also believed that *wasabi* disguises any unpleasant flavours of the raw fish.)

Wasabi is also delicious served with grilled meats and chicken. A touch of *wasabi* mixed with Japanese rice vinegar and a light peanut oil makes a delicious dressing for mixed green salads or steamed vegetables. Try spreading a small dab of *wasabi* on prawns, fish fillets or raw oysters before grilling.

MAKING YOUR OWN HOT SAUCES

If you have friends who love hot, peppery foods, these hot sauces make ideal gifts. Simply place the sauce in a clean jar or bottle and write out a label describing the contents of the sauce, with a warning of just how hot it really is.

Nam Prik **(Thai Hot Sauce)**

This recipe comes from Jennifer Brennan's *The Original Thai Cookbook* (Richard Marek Publishers, 1981). Serve it with fish, noodle dishes, chicken and grilled meat. The sauce keeps well for several weeks, refrigerated, and even tastes better after a day or so.

    2 tablespoons whole, dried shrimp, chopped
    6 cloves garlic, chopped
    4 dried red chilli peppers (including seeds), chopped
    1 teaspoon granulated sugar
    3 tablespoons fish sauce (*nam pla*) (see page 103)
    3 tablespoons lime juice
    2 fresh red or green serrano chillies, seeded and
    finely chopped

In a mortar or food processor, pound or grind the shrimp, garlic, dried chillies and sugar until the mixture is well blended. Gradually add the fish sauce and lime juice, a spoonful at a time, until you have a smooth mixture. Pour in a serving bowl and stir in the fresh chillies. *Makes about 120 ml/4 fl oz.*

Chinese Chilli and Black Bean Sauce

Chilli peppers, black beans, sesame oil, garlic, ginger and Szechuan peppercorns all go into making this thick, spicy sauce. Serve it with dumplings, stir-fried vegetables, seafood and Chinese noodle dishes.

    40 g/1½ oz chilli powder
    2 cloves garlic

1 tablespoon Chinese black beans, rinsed and finely
chopped
2½ tablespoons sesame oil
2 tablespoons peanut oil
1½ teaspoons chopped fresh ginger
5 Szechuan or black peppercorns
1 small dried red chilli pepper, chopped with seeds
1 spring onion, chopped

In a small serving bowl, mix the chilli powder, garlic and black
beans and reserve.

In a small frying pan, heat the sesame and peanut oil over a
high heat. Add the ginger, peppercorns, chilli pepper and spring
onion and cook for about 3–4 minutes, or until the ginger and
spring onion begin to turn golden brown. Remove the frying pan
from the heat and leave to cool for a few minutes.

Strain the flavoured oil over the chilli mixture, discarding the
ginger, peppercorns, chilli and spring onion, and stir to form a
smooth, thick sauce. Leave the sauce to stand for about 30
minutes before serving, or place in a clean, clear jar and cover and
store in a cool place for up to four months. *Makes about
120 ml/4 fl oz.*

Harissa

The fire-engine-red colour of *harissa* is a sign of what's to come;
when freshly made, *harissa* is hotter than hot. (You'll be screaming for the fire extinguisher.) But once it's given a chance to stand
for a while, the flavours of the lemon juice and cumin mixed with
the chilli create a wonderfully unique condiment.

Used sparingly, *harissa* adds zest to *couscous*, stews, soups and
casseroles; it's also great served with thin slices of cold lamb or
beef. Mix a bit into a home-made mayonnaise to make a spicy dip
for cold prawns and raw vegetables.

75 g/3 oz dried red chilli peppers
2 teaspoons salt
2 cloves garlic
about 2 tablespoons lemon juice
1 teaspoon ground cumin powder
olive oil

79

Place the chillies in a medium saucepan and cover with cold water. Place over a high heat and allow the water to come to the boil. Remove from the heat and leave for about 1 hour.

Drain the chillies and place in a blender or food processor with the salt and garlic. Blend the mixture and add the lemon juice, bit by bit, to keep the mixture moving. (If the peppers don't seem to be blending, add additional lemon juice as needed.) Once the mixture is thoroughly blended, remove and place in a small glass jar. Stir in the cumin and smooth the mixture down. Pour enough olive oil over the *harissa* to cover the top completely. Cover and refrigerate. *Makes about 120 ml/4 fl oz.*

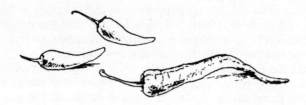

Moroccan Hot Sauce

This is an adaptation of a traditional Moroccan hot pepper sauce called Sauce Chermella. If you like the musty, exotic flavour of cumin, then you'll love this peppery mixture. It goes well with all sorts of barbecued foods, with *couscous*, as a marinade for chicken, prawn, swordfish or lamb, and as a dipping sauce for raw vegetables and avocados. One of the best ways to eat this hot sauce is in a toasted pitta bread sandwich filled with thinly sliced barbecued lamb.

½ teaspoon cayenne pepper
1 teaspoon peanut oil
2 cloves garlic, chopped
1 small fresh chilli pepper, stemmed and with seeds
1½ tablespoons fresh, chopped coriander
1 tablespoon cumin powder
1½ teaspoons paprika
1 teaspoon salt
2 tablespoons red wine vinegar
1½ tablespoons water
2½ tablespoons olive oil

In a small bowl, mix the cayenne pepper and the oil and leave at room temperature for 30 minutes. Place all the remaining ingredients except the olive oil in a blender or food processor and blend until smooth. Add the cayenne pepper oil and the olive oil, a teaspoon at a time, until the sauce is smooth and slightly thickened. Transfer the sauce to a small stainless steel saucepan and boil for 2–3 minutes over a high heat. Remove the pan from the heat and let the sauce cool slightly. Place in a clean jar and refrigerate. Serve cold or at room temperature. *Makes about 120 ml/4 fl oz.*

Salsa Picante (Hot Sauce)

This Mexican *salsa* is spiked with the fresh, distinctive flavour of fresh coriander. When freshly made, it is hot – as in VERY HOT. The longer it stands, the more subdued its fire becomes; it is best served within a few hours. Serve as a dip with taco chips and guacamole or as a condiment with tortillas, grilled meats and eggs.

4 large, ripe tomatoes, chopped
3 spring onions, thinly sliced
2 tablespoons chopped fresh coriander leaves
2½ tablespoons fresh lime juice
2 fresh jalapeño or serrano chillies, trimmed and chopped (with seeds)
1 large clove garlic, chopped
120 ml/4 fl oz water
salt to taste

In a large bowl, mix the tomatoes, spring onions, coriander and lime juice and set aside.
In a blender or food processor, blend the chillies and garlic until finely chopped. Add the water and process for another 2–3 seconds until well blended. Add the chilli and garlic sauce to the tomato mixture and mix well; add salt to taste. Refrigerate and serve. *Makes about 750 ml/1¼ pints.*

Salsa Cruda

This is a really versatile *salsa*. It goes with any type of barbecued food, fried prawns and chicken or on grilled fish. It also makes a great dip for *nachos* or taco chips with guacamole.

120 g/4½ oz very ripe fresh tomatoes, coarsely chopped
2 tablespoons fresh lime juice
2–3 tablespoons finely chopped jalapeño or serrano chilli peppers
1 small onion, coarsely chopped

Mix all the ingredients and leave to stand for 1 hour. This sauce is best used within 6 hours; the longer it stands, the less intense and crunchy it becomes. *Makes about 250 ml/8 fl oz.*

Mission-Style *Salsa*

I first tasted this incredibly hot *salsa* at a party in New York given for a friend who was leaving for Latin America. Robert Huff sent me his recipe along with the following notes: 'Fresh *cilantro* (coriander) is an essential ingredient in this recipe. It provides a cooling, earthy relief from the hot peppers. Salsa can be spooned on eggs, steak and barbecued foods. It is more often served as a dip with corn chips or taco chips. *Salsa* is high in vitamin C. In Los Angeles, *salsa*, taco chips and shots of tequila are touted as being an effective cold remedy. A good *salsa* should always make you sweat.' *This recipe makes enough for a crowd.*

10 fresh plum tomatoes, peeled and coarsely chopped
250 g/9 oz canned tomatoes, coarsely chopped
8 cloves garlic, minced
2 medium onions, one minced and one coarsely chopped
6 spring onions, thinly sliced
1 large green pepper, coarsely chopped
3–4 fresh green chilli peppers, coarsely chopped with seeds
5 jalapeño peppers, coarsely chopped with seeds

8 serrano peppers, coarsely chopped with seeds
3 tablespoons chopped fresh coriander
120 ml/4 fl oz red wine vinegar
4 tablespoons olive oil
½ teaspoon cayenne pepper
½ teaspoon freshly ground black pepper

Mix all the ingredients in a large bowl and leave to stand for 30 minutes before serving. *Makes about 1.5 litres/2½ pints.*

Brazilian Hot Pepper and Lemon Sauce

This very spicy, very sour sauce is an adaptation of the Brazilian sauce, *Môlho de Pimenta e Limão*. It is traditionally served with *feijoada* (the national dish of Brazil) – a feast of smoked and fresh meats, black beans, Brazilian rice, greens and orange slices. It is also excellent with grilled meats, pork and prawns. Make the sauce just before serving; it tends to lose its crunchy texture after a few hours.

5 finely chopped bottled, pickled tabasco peppers,
plus ¼ teaspoon of the vinegar
120 ml/4 fl oz lemon juice
1 small onion, finely chopped
2 cloves garlic, finely chopped
1 tablespoon parsley, finely chopped

Mix all the ingredients in a small serving bowl. Leave to stand, uncovered, at room temperature, for about 15 minutes before serving. *Makes about 250 ml/8 fl oz.*

Sherry Peppers Sauce

Flavouring dry sherry with chilli peppers is an old Bermudian tradition. In just about every restaurant on the island, small bottles of this hot, spicy condiment are served. You can buy bottled sherry peppers sauce, but it's really easy to make your own. If you make this sauce in an old preserving jar or glass bottle it makes a great gift.

Use it in soups, chowders, marinades and barbecue sauces or

sprinkled over fried eggs and pan-fried fish. A dash of sherry peppers sauce in a rich seafood chowder is an incredible taste sensation. Plan on letting the sauce steep for at least two weeks before using.

4 fresh red or green chilli peppers (you can use any type of pepper you want, depending on just how hot you want the sauce to be)
2 small dried red chilli peppers
450 ml/¾ pint dry sherry

Place all of the peppers in a clean, clear bottle or preserving jar and cover with the sherry. Seal tightly and allow to steep for at least two weeks before using. After two weeks, taste the sauce. Be careful, it will be hot – very hot. You can leave the peppers in (which will cause the sauce to get hotter, though not too much hotter) or strain them out at this point. Keep in a dark, cool spot. *Makes about 450 ml/¾ pint.*

Freshly Grated Horseradish

Making fresh horseradish can be a painful, tearful, sinus-clearing experience. The traditional way to do it is to grate the fresh horseradish root by hand. If you choose this method, be sure to have plenty of tissues around. An easier way to make freshly grated horseradish is in a blender or food processor. But this, you should be warned, has its risks, too. Do not stick your head over the blender to see how the horseradish is doing; the fumes from the horseradish root are so intense that a coughing fit is virtually guaranteed. Use a spatula to stir the horseradish around and check on its texture. Now that you've been told of all the possible dangers, enjoy. Freshly grated horseradish is a spicy, pungent treat that is definitely worth the effort.

75 g/3 oz peeled, diced horseradish (you can use either a peeler or a small, sharp knife to peel the horseradish root)
about 4 tablespoons white wine or cider vinegar (never measure vinegar in a metal container; always use a glass or porcelain measuring cup)
salt to taste

84

Place the horseradish in a blender or food processor and blend until thoroughly grated, about 5–6 seconds. If you're going to serve the horseradish right away (and if you like it strong and straight), stop here. If, however, you want to store it for future use (and if you like a creamy-style horseradish), add the vinegar to the blender, 1 tablespoon at a time, until it reaches the desired consistency. Taste for seasoning (watch out), and stir in the salt to taste. Place in a small, clear bottle or jar and refrigerate. Use within three to four weeks. *Makes about 120 ml/4 fl oz.*

Fresh Horseradish with Beetroot (Red Horseradish)

Fresh beetroot not only gives horseradish a beautiful pinkish-red colour but they also add a delicious, natural sweetness.

Follow the above recipe and add 50–75 g/2–3 oz of freshly cooked diced beetroot to the blender with the diced horseradish. *Makes about 175 ml/6 fl oz.*

COOKING WITH HOT PEPPER SAUCES AND HORSERADISH

Swordfish with Horseradish-Thyme Butter

In this recipe, the milk and the natural fish juice create a creamy sauce, and the horseradish butter provides a sharp, spicy contrast.

450 g/1 lb swordfish steak, cut about 2.5 cm/1 in thick
120 ml/4 fl oz milk
65 g/2½ oz unsalted butter
1½ tablespoons prepared white horseradish
1 tablespoon fresh lemon juice
2 sprigs thyme, or ¼ teaspoon dried thyme
1 lemon, cut into wedges

Place the swordfish in a small baking tin. Pour the milk over the fish and marinate, covered, for about 1½ hours.

Preheat the oven to 180°C/350°F/Gas Mark 4. In a small saucepan, melt the butter over a moderate heat. Add the horseradish, lemon juice and thyme. Cook, stirring, until slightly thickened, about 3 minutes. Spoon the horseradish butter over the swordfish and bake for 15 minutes, or until just tender when tested with a fork. Place under the grill until golden brown, bubbling and opaque throughout, about 4–5 minutes. Serve with lemon wedges. *Serves 2–3.*

Devilish Oysters

These oysters – grilled with hot pepper sauce and a touch of fresh breadcrumbs – make an excellent first course or hors d'oeuvre. Keep the shells after you've opened the oysters; you may want to serve the oysters in their shells after they've been grilled.

You can use any type of hot pepper sauce or *sambal* you want with this recipe; the Chinese chilli sauces on page 68 are particularly good.

12 opened oysters, with 2½ tablespoons of juice
about ¼–2 teaspoons of hot pepper sauce
1½ teaspoons fresh breadcrumbs

Preheat the grill. Place the oysters with the juice in a small, shallow casserole. Drizzle a few drops of the hot sauce over each oyster; ½ teaspoon makes the oysters mildly hot and 2 teaspoons is 'watch-out' hot. Top each oyster with breadcrumbs and place under the grill for 4–5 minutes, or until cooked and tender.

Place the oysters back in their shells or serve them straight out of the casserole. *Serves 2–3.*

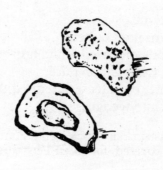

Soured Cream, Horseradish and Caper Sauce

Serve this simple, piquant sauce with smoked fish or smoked ham. It's also delicious with roast beef or as a dip for beef fondue or raw vegetables.

    250 ml/8 fl oz soured cream
    2 tablespoons freshly grated horseradish, or 3
    tablespoons drained bottled horseradish
    2 tablespoons capers, drained
    1 teaspoon Tabasco or hot pepper sauce

Mix together the soured cream, horseradish and capers and add the Tabasco to taste. Refrigerate and serve cold. *Makes 250 ml/8 fl oz.*

Horseradish Butter

This pungent butter is delicious added to steamed new potatoes, grilled fish or beef. You can make it with either white or red (beetroot) horseradish, depending on what it's being served with. The bright colour of the red horseradish butter is fantastic with pan-fried fillet of sole, boiled new potatoes or grilled salmon.

    100 g/4 oz salted butter, at room temperature
    2 tablespoons freshly grated horseradish, or 3
    tablespoons drained prepared horseradish
    1 teaspoon freshly ground black pepper

87

Using the back of a wooden spoon, cream the butter until light and fluffy. Stir in the horseradish and pepper.

Spread a tablespoon of flour over your hands and on a clean work surface. Form the butter into a log shape and wrap in waxed paper. Refrigerate or freeze and slice off a tablespoon at a time as needed. *Makes about 100 g/4 oz.*

The Beach Plum Inn's Horseradish Sauce

The Beach Plum Inn, in Menemsha on Martha's Vineyard, Massachusetts, serves this delicious sauce on top of a cold medallion of beef salad. Bibb (or Boston) lettuce leaves are arranged on a serving plate and topped with thinly sliced, slightly rare medallions of beef. The horseradish sauce can be served on top of the beef or on the side.

> 250 ml/8 fl oz double cream
> 3 tablespoons prepared horseradish, drained
> 2 tablespoons lemon juice
> ½ teaspoon salt
> about ¼ teaspoon Tabasco sauce
> ¼ teaspoon white pepper

Whip the cream until it forms peaks. Gently fold in the horseradish, lemon juice, salt, Tabasco and pepper. Taste for seasoning and add additional Tabasco sauce if desired. Refrigerate and serve. *Makes about 250 ml/8 fl oz.*

5

Occidental (or Western) Sauces

Ketchup, Mayonnaise, Steak Sauce,
Worcestershire Sauce, Cranberry Sauce,
Cumberland Sauce

OCCIDENTAL SAUCES ARE familiar to most Americans, but their histories are surprisingly exotic. Who would have thought, for instance, that ketchup originated in China, was imported to England and then popularised in the United States? Or that mayonnaise is based on a Spanish garlic sauce and Worcestershire sauce on an ancient Roman recipe?

OCCIDENTAL SAUCE SURVEY

Over the years, these sauces have become an integral part of the American diet. Most of them are now considered everyday 'supermarket sauces,' but recently a number of new, updated renditions have surfaced in speciality food shops.

Ketchup

The Americans are a nation in which the average man, woman and child consumes 1¾ gallons of ketchup a year. They use ketchup to spice up their hamburgers, hot dogs, chips, and even their politics. It was only a few years ago that President Reagan created a national controversy by declaring ketchup a legitimate vegetable for school lunches. The Reagan policy provided a rare opportunity for food critics and welfare mothers to get together on an issue. Both knew the ultimate truth – ketchup is a condiment, *not* a vegetable.

There are several explanations about the derivation of the word 'ketchup.' Some historians say it was named after *kechap*, a tangy sauce made in Malaysia and Singapore; others claim it comes from the Siamese word *kachiap* or the Indonesian word *ketjap*, meaning a sauce added to food for extra flavour. But the most widely accepted story attributes the word to the Chinese. *The Oxford Dictionary of English Etymology* lists the word 'ketchup' as early as 1690 and shows it to be of Chinese origin.

The story goes that in the mid-seventeenth century English sailors discovered the Chinese using a pungent sauce made of fish entrails and brine called *ke tsiap*. The sailors had a need for products that would hold up during long sea voyages, and an even stronger need for sauces that would spice up their monotonous diet while on board ship. They took *ke tsiap* back to England. But once they got home and tried to recreate the sauce, the idea of fish entrails seemed less and less appealing. So English cooks experimented with the recipe using more conventional ingredients.

Walnut, oyster and mushroom ketchups were particularly popular. In 1748, Mrs Harrison wrote in her popular *Housekeeper's Pocketbook* that 'no good British homemaker should ever be without the pungent condiment.'

Ketchup eventually made its way to the United States in the latter part of the seventeenth century. It is said that cooks from Maine were the first to invent a tomato-based ketchup. Maine sea captains who travelled to Mexico and the Spanish West Indies brought tomato seeds back with them and planted the seeds with great success. The result was a spicy, pungent sauce that is still served throughout New England with baked beans, fish cakes and meat.

Before tomato ketchup caught on across the whole country, there were a number of other ketchups that characterised early American cooking. Regional cooks made the popular sauce using whatever ingredients happened to be in abundance. The early Shakers, for instance, made ketchup from apples, cucumbers, gooseberries and grapes.

In 1861, Isabella Beeton wrote in her popular guide, *Mrs Beeton's Book of Household Management*, 'This flavouring, if genuine and well prepared, is one of the most useful sauces to the experienced cook, and no trouble should be spared in its preparation.' Up until the late 1800s, it was commonplace for American housewives to spend hours over a hot wood stove simmering up pots of home-made ketchup.

Then in 1876, Mr Henry Heinz had a brainstorm. The rest is history. Ketchup is now commercially made and consumed the world over, but it is ultimately considered an all-American condiment.

TASTING NOTES:

Americans love to eat ketchup with just about everything. Hamburgers and chips are traditional, but ketchup also gets poured onto hot dogs, steaks, chops – even baked potatoes.

We tend to think of ketchup as an ordinary, everyday sauce, but when I was in France a few years ago I was amazed to find it in some of the finest speciality food shops. It seems that in some parts of France, ketchup is being marketed as a kind of trendy American sauce. At the Ritz Hotel in Paris, the head chef makes an elegant sweetbread and vegetable salad served with a ketchup-based vinaigrette.

Ketchup is delicious in baked beans, stews, as a base for barbecue sauce (see page 100 for recipe), marinades and spicy cocktail sauces. A tablespoon of ketchup whisked into a vinaigrette is wonderful served with ripe tomatoes and thick slices of red onion.

Mayonnaise

There are few sauces considered more American than mayonnaise. But, like many American foods, this egg-and-oil-based sauce has its roots in an old European recipe. There are several theories about the origin of mayonnaise, the most popular being that it is based on *alioli*, a Spanish garlic sauce that dates back hundreds of years.

It is believed that some time in the seventeenth century, the French cardinal and statesman Richelieu visited Mahón, the capital of the Balearic island of Minorca, and tasted *alioli*. He was so impressed by the garlic sauce that he brought the recipe back to France. There, French chefs experimented with the sauce, eliminating the garlic and replacing it with the tart, lighter flavour of fresh lemon juice. They named their creation *sauce Mahónnaise*, but in time it was changed to mayonnaise.

Exactly when mayonnaise made its way to the United States isn't clearly documented, but it has been commercially manufactured in that country for quite some time. Inside a stack of old cookbooks I bought at a country auction a few years ago, I found a calendar and recipe booklet, published by the Hellmann's Mayonnaise Company, that dates back to 1926. The calendar is filled with wonderful vintage recipes like tutti-frutti salad, jellied vegetable mould and (get this) peanut butter and olive sandwiches with mayonnaise. But the best part of the calendar is the introduction: 'Mayonnaise dressing has been known for centuries . . . Ever since it was first made, mayonnaise has been considered a great delicacy and one which required a great skill and art and

91

patience to prepare successfully at home. . . .'

I was amazed to see that, as early as 1926, Americans were being 'brainwashed' into believing that making mayonnaise at home is a time-consuming and difficult task. Granted, bottled mayonnaise was seen by many as a time-saving convenience but, over the years, it has come to mean a mediocre, fairly tasteless condiment. The fact of the matter is that it's incredibly easy to make delicious, fresh-tasting mayonnaise; see recipe on page 97.

TASTING NOTES:
Serve mayonnaise with sandwiches and cold meat platters, in salads and coleslaw. Use as the base for flavoured sauces; see pages 98–9 for ideas. You can also use home-made mayonnaise to make tartare sauce; see recipe on page 99.

Although nothing can beat a home-made mayonnaise, there are now a number of sauces sold in supermarkets, and health and speciality food shops that are worth eating.

Steak Sauces

The popularity of Worcestershire sauce (see this page) in the mid-1800s inspired many variations, most of which were sauces created to be served with steak. I have never understood the appeal of steak sauce. Buying an expensive cut of beef and then pouring a sweet sauce over it just doesn't make sense to me. Obviously there are a lot of people who disagree; steak sauce is a big seller almost everywhere.

Worcestershire Sauce

It's black and rich, pungent and salty. Its flavour is almost meaty, but there's also a slight hint of fish. It tastes as good in a Bloody Mary as it does on a hamburger. Many people can't spell it, but almost everyone has tried it. It is, in a word, unique.

Worcestershire sauce has been popular since the 1830s. But just how old the recipe is, no one is exactly sure. A variation of Worcestershire is said to date back to the ancient Romans, who made a sauce of salted fish called *garum*.

The people at Lea & Perrins (makers of the world's best-selling Worcestershire sauce) have their own explanation about the origins of Worcestershire. Their story goes something like this: In 1830, Lord Sandys, Governor General of Bengal, discovered a recipe for a pungent Indian sauce and brought it back to England.

He gave the recipe to two druggists, John Lea and William Perrins. They tasted the sauce and found it to be absolutely awful so they immediately dumped the sauce into a few wooden barrels in their basement and forgot all about it. Years later, they remembered the sauce and went downstairs to discard it. But first, they decided to give it another taste. And, lo and behold, this awful concoction had developed a fantastic flavour.

Lea & Perrins named the sauce Worcestershire because it was made in the shire of Worcester. Since the sauce kept so well and actually developed flavour as it aged, it became popular on board ship. Sailors used liberal amounts of the sauce to disguise the rancid taste of their food. Before long, Worcestershire sauce became popular worldwide.

Today *Lea & Perrins Worcestershire Sauce* is made using the chemists' original recipe. Anchovies, soybeans, tamarind, vinegar, garlic, shallots, molasses and spices are mixed in enormous wooden vats. The sauce is allowed to age for two years before being pressed and strained. It is then placed in its distinctive glass bottle and wrapped in the traditional Lea & Perrins brown paper.

TASTING NOTES:

Worcestershire sauce adds a great flavour to marinades and other sauces, but it's best used as a table condiment. Splash it on burgers and steaks, eggs, fried fish, baked clams and grilled cheese sandwiches.

Lea & Perrins is the most famous, but there are also a number of other good brands of Worcestershire sauce available.

Other Occidental Sauces

Cranberry Sauce is an American tradition. I love it, but wonder why it is that we only eat it at holiday time. See page 94 for a recipe you can make when fresh cranberries are in season and then freeze and enjoy year-round.

Cumberland Sauce is a sweet, slightly spicy mixture of red currant jelly, dry port wine, oranges and spices. According to Elizabeth David's *Spices, Salts and Aromatics in the English Kitchen*, '[Cumberland sauce] was named after Ernest, Duke of Cumberland', and is 'probably German in origin'.

The sauce became popular in England in the early 1800s. Initially, it was found only in the kitchens of the aristocracy but was soon made popular by the famous French chef, Auguste Escoffier. Cumberland sauce was originally created to be served with boar's head, but it also goes well with more common foods like roast lamb, beef, venison, ham and tongue. Fortnum & Mason make a wonderful Cumberland sauce, but the best is home-made; see recipe on page 95.

In eighteenth-century England, dozens of new sauces were created to improve the flavour of meats, game and fish. *Harvey Sauce* was reputedly invented by Peter Harvey, host of the Black Dog Inn in Middlesex. The main ingredients are anchovies, walnut pickles, soy sauce, malt vinegar, garlic and spices. Like its rival, Worcestershire sauce, Harvey's is aged for several years and then strained to create a clear, rich sauce.

It's a dark, fairly thin condiment that is delicious in soups and stews and served with meats, game and poultry.

Mint Sauce is another British favourite. It is traditionally served with leg of lamb or grilled lamb chops. But mint sauce is also wonderful with roast beef, pork, chicken, ground lamb burgers and curries. (See page 127 for information on mint jellies.)

Mint sauce is easy to make: Simply place 2 tablespoons finely chopped fresh mint in a bowl or jar. Boil 5 tablespoons white wine vinegar in a stainless steel pan with 1 tablespoon of white or brown sugar. Pour over the mint and leave for 2–3 hours before serving.

MAKING YOUR OWN OCCIDENTAL SAUCES

Lucy's Cranberry-Orange-Maple Sauce

Make this delicious sauce in the autumn when cranberries are in season, and then freeze it so you can enjoy it all the year round.

Serve with roast turkey, chicken, duck or ham, or spooned over baked or puréed squash. It's also delicious with ice cream and butter cookies.

250 g/9 oz caster sugar
450 ml/¾ pint water
450 g/1 lb fresh cranberries
5 tablespoons freshly squeezed orange juice
4 tablespoons maple syrup
1 tablespoon grated orange rind
1 tablespoon coarsely chopped candied ginger, or ¼ teaspoon grated fresh ginger

In a large saucepan, mix the sugar with the water and simmer over a moderately high heat for about 5 minutes, or until the liquid becomes slightly syrupy. Add the cranberries and simmer for another 5 minutes, or until the berries begin to pop open. Add the orange juice, maple syrup, orange rind and ginger and simmer for another 2–3 minutes.

Pour the sauce into hot, sterilised jars and store in the refrigerator or freezer. *Makes about 1.2 litres/2 pints.*

Cumberland Sauce

    300 g/11 oz red currant or blackcurrant jelly
    2 tablespoons very thinly sliced orange rind
    2 tablespoons orange juice
    1 tablespoon sugar
    1½ teaspoons powdered mustard
    ¾ teaspoon ground ginger
    pinch of salt
    pinch of black pepper
    120 ml/4 fl oz dry port

Heat the jelly, orange rind and juice, sugar, mustard, ginger, salt and pepper in a saucepan over a moderate heat for 5 minutes. Stir occasionally to dissolve the mustard and ginger. Add the port and simmer for 5–10 minutes, or until slightly thickened. Allow to cool and refrigerate. Serve cold. *Makes about 425 g/15 oz.*

Home-made Tomato Ketchup

You'll need lots of fresh, ripe tomatoes for this ketchup. The best time to make this is in August, when your garden (or your local market) is overflowing with ripe, inexpensive tomatoes. This ketchup takes some time to make but the results are definitely worth it; you may never use bottled ketchup again.

4.5 kg/10 lb ripe tomatoes, chopped
1 large red onion, thinly sliced
250 ml/8 fl oz apple cider vinegar
175–225 g/6–8 oz brown or white sugar
2 tablespoons salt
1 teaspoon cayenne pepper
1 teaspoon ground cinnamon
1 teaspoon ground allspice
1 teaspon baking powder
¼ teaspoon freshly grated nutmeg

Place the tomatoes and the onion in a large stainless steel saucepan and place over a moderate heat for 30 minutes, or until the tomatoes are soft and have broken down. Strain the mixture through a large sieve, making sure to stir as much of the pulp through as possible. (Don't worry if the liquid seems very watery; it will thicken later.)

Return the strained tomatoes to the saucepan and whisk in the remaining ingredients. Let the mixture simmer over a moderate heat for 1½–2 hours, stirring occasionally, until the mixture has thickened to the consistency of ketchup. Place in sterilised jars and refrigerate; it will keep for several months. If you want to double the recipe and preserve the ketchup, process in a boiling water bath for 20 minutes (see page 129 for additional notes on bottling). *Makes 1–1.5 litres/1¾–2½ pints.*

Quick Ketchup

This slightly spicy ketchup, created by Penny Potenz Winship of New York City, is terrific for people who are watching their weight or their sodium intake. It is made in a blender without salt or sugar and tastes as good (if not better) than anything you'll ever find in the shops. If tightly covered and refrigerated, it will keep for months.

1 medium onion, chopped
½ clove of garlic
5 tablespoons frozen apple juice concentrate
175 g/6 oz tomato purée
120 ml/4 fl oz malt vinegar
½ teaspoon cayenne pepper
¼ teaspoon ground cinnamon
pinch of ground cloves

Place the onion, garlic and apple juice concentrate in a blender and purée until smooth. Add the remaining ingredients and blend until smooth. Keep in an airtight bottle or jar and refrigerate. *Makes about 250 ml/8 fl oz.*

Basic Home-made Mayonnaise

There have been volumes written about the 'best' recipe for mayonnaise (some claiming that it *must* be made from olive oil, others arguing that it has to be a light vegetable oil). I have no intention of adding to that long-running debate. The point is to start making your own mayonnaise at home; it's cheap, easy and tastes a lot better than most bottled varieties.

Many people like to make mayonnaise in a blender or food processor. I've always preferred to make mayonnaise with a whisk or a hand-held electric beater so that I can watch the process. You have a lot more control over the texture and consistency of your mayonnaise if you can see it thicken, bit by bit.

Use whatever type of oil you like with this recipe. I prefer a richly flavoured mayonnaise and use either all olive oil or 175 ml/6 fl oz olive oil and 4 tablespoons light vegetable oil. Whatever you choose, make sure all your ingredients (plus your bowl and whisk) are at room temperature. If your ingredients are too hot or cold the sauce won't hold together.

2 egg yolks, at room temperature
1 teaspoon Dijon mustard
1½ tablespoons lemon juice
½ teaspoon salt
¼ teaspoon pepper, preferably white
250 ml/8 fl oz olive, peanut, safflower or vegetable oil
1 tablespoon white wine vinegar

In a large bowl, whisk the yolks by hand or with an electric beater until they begin to thicken slightly and turn a light lemon colour. Whisk in the mustard, 1 tablespoon of the lemon juice, and the salt and pepper. Gradually add 120 ml/4 fl oz of the oil, a few drops at a time, making sure that each drop has been incorporated before adding the next.

At this stage, the sauce should begin to thicken and hold together. You can relax and add the remaining oil in a *slow*, steady stream. When almost all the oil has been added, whisk in the vinegar and the remaining ½ tablespoon of the lemon juice. Taste for seasoning and adjust, if needed. If the mayonnaise doesn't seem to be holding together, add a tablespoon of boiling water and whisk until the sauce comes together. (See note for further hints.) Don't be concerned if the mayonnaise seems a bit thin, it will thicken a bit in the refrigerator. Refrigerate the mayonnaise in a glass jar or covered bowl for at least a few hours before serving; use within 5 days. *Makes about 250 ml/8 fl oz.*

Note: If your mayonnaise begins to separate, don't panic. There's a simple way to save it: whisk an egg yolk in a bowl until it turns a light lemon colour. Then, gradually whisk into the separated mayonnaise until the sauce thickens and holds together.

Flavoured Mayonnaise

Once you've mastered the basic recipe for mayonnaise you can make all sorts of wonderful sauces. Listed here are a few of my favourites.

Lemon-Curry Mayonnaise: To 250 ml/8 fl oz of home-made mayonnaise, whisk in 2 tablespoons lemon juice, 2 teaspoons curry powder and 1 teaspoon cumin powder. Serve with a prawn and potato salad, a cold mussel or tuna salad or a cold beef and spring onion salad. It's also delicious on a cold lamb open sandwich or with devilled eggs.

Green Herb Mayonnaise: When making the basic mayonnaise recipe, substitute 1 tablespoon herb-flavoured vinegar for the white wine vinegar. To 250 ml/8 fl oz home-made mayonnaise, stir in 3 tablespoons finely chopped assorted fresh herbs (tarragon, basil, chives, rosemary, parsley or thyme). Serve with a cold seafood salad, poached salmon, cold pasta salad, chicken salad or on a sandwich of ripe tomato slices and red onion on dark rye bread.

Garlic Mayonnaise: To 250 ml/8 fl oz of home-made mayonnaise, add 4–6 cloves of garlic mashed with ¼ teaspoon salt and 1 tablespoon fresh lemon juice. Serve with a cold seafood salad, grilled prawns, mixed vegetable salad, fish stew, roast beef and roast chicken.

Mustard Mayonnaise: To 250 ml/8 fl oz home-made mayonnaise, whisk in 50 g/2 oz strong Dijon mustard. Serve on sandwiches, with cold meat salads, turkey salad, cold tongue and in coleslaw.

Sesame-Ginger Mayonnaise: To 250 ml/8 fl oz home-made mayonnaise, mix in 2 teaspoons Oriental sesame oil and 1 tablespoon grated fresh ginger. Use with chicken, turkey or prawn salad, as a dip for raw vegetables and grilled prawns, or on a sliced chicken and tomato open sandwich.

Horseradish Mayonnaise: To 250 ml/8 fl oz home-made mayonnaise, add 2½ tablespoons prepared horseradish. If you like it hotter, add an additional ½ tablespoon. Horseradish with grated beetroot gives the mayonnaise a beautiful reddish-pink colour. Serve with potato salad, coleslaw, cold roast beef and lamb, and with sandwiches.

Lime Mayonnaise: When making the basic mayonnaise recipe, substitute 2 tablespoons fresh lime juice for the lemon juice and vinegar. Serve this mayonnaise with baked salmon, grilled swordfish, cold boiled prawns or in a turkey or chicken sandwich.

Nut Oil Mayonnaise: To 250 ml/8 fl oz home-made mayonnaise, add 1½–2 tablespoons walnut, hazelnut or almond oil. Serve with sandwiches and in salads.

Tartare Sauce

I have never tasted a bottled tartare sauce I thought was really terrific. However, it's easy to make. Serve this sauce with fried clams, oysters or fish fillets.

250 ml/8 fl oz mayonnaise, preferably home-made
1½ tablespoons tarragon-flavoured vinegar, or white
wine vinegar
½ tablespoon lemon juice
150 g/5 oz finely chopped pickles or *cornichons* (see
page 126 for explanation)
4 tablespoons minced onions
2 tablespoons capers, drained
1½ tablespoons minced parsley
1 tablespoon finely chopped chives
1 teaspoon mustard powder
¼ teaspoon salt
pinch of cayenne pepper
1 hard-boiled egg, finely chopped, optional

In a medium-size bowl, mix the mayonnaise with the remaining ingredients. Stir well to make sure that the mustard is thoroughly dissolved. Refrigerate and serve cold. *Makes about 350 ml/12 fl oz.*

COOKING WITH OCCIDENTAL SAUCES

Bill Bell's Barbecue Sauce

This is a quick, easy barbecue sauce that is delicious with chicken, steak, ribs, or even tofu. You can make it as hot and spicy as you want; add the Tabasco to taste.

250 ml/8 fl oz home-made tomato ketchup (see page
96), or 250 ml/8 fl oz bottled ketchup
about 1 tablespoon Tabasco or other hot pepper
sauce to taste
3 tablespoons honey or maple syrup
1½ tablespoons minced fresh garlic

In a large bowl, mix all the ingredients. Taste for seasoning; if you want a very hot sauce, add an additional tablespoon of Tabasco. Add to chicken, meat or tofu; leave to marinate for a few hours and barbecue. *Makes about 300 ml/½ pint.*

Marinated Chickens' Livers, Apricot and Prune Kebabs

This ketchup-based marinade adds an incredibly good flavour to chickens' livers, apricots and prunes. Serve these savoury kebabs on triangles of buttered toast as a first course or an hors d'oeuvre.

(You can also use this marinade with steak, lamb or chicken. Triple the recipe and let the meat or poultry marinate for about an hour and then grill or barbecue.)

THE MARINADE
2 tablespoons ketchup
1 tablespoon Worcestershire sauce
1 tablespoon vegetable oil
2 teaspoons Dijon mustard
2 teaspoons anchovy purée

THE KEBABS
12 chickens' livers, cut in half
12 dried apricots
12 stoned prunes
12 rashers of bacon, each cut into 4 pieces
24 bay leaves

In a small bowl, combine the marinade ingredients. Add the livers, toss, and allow to marinate for about 1 hour.

Meanwhile, place the apricots and prunes in a small saucepan with water to cover. Over a high heat, bring the water to the boil; reduce heat and poach the fruit until tender but not mushy, about 2–3 minutes. Drain, cool and cut each piece of fruit in half.

Preheat the grill. Wrap each piece of fruit in a piece of bacon. Dip the bay leaves in the marinade. Onto each of twelve 18 cm/7 in skewers, thread 1 wrapped apricot, 1 bay leaf, 1 piece of chickens' liver and a wrapped prune, followed by another apricot, bay leaf, chickens' liver and prune. Grill the kebabs about 10 cm/4 in from the heat for 2 minutes on each side, or until the bacon is crisp. *Serves 4–6.*

Chicken Salad in a Curry-Chutney Mayonnaise with Grapes and Almonds

THE MAYONNAISE
350 ml/12 fl oz home-made mayonnaise (see recipe on page 97)
2 tablespoons mango chutney, finely chopped (see recipe on page 144)
1 tablespoon curry powder
pinch of ground cumin
pinch of cayenne pepper
1 tablespoon dry white wine
1 tablespoon lemon juice
salt and pepper to taste

THE SALAD
1 roasted or poached chicken, about 1.5 kg/3½ lb
15 g/½ oz unsalted butter
100 g/4 oz almonds (flaked)
450 g/1 lb seedless green grapes
1 bunch watercress

Make the mayonnaise: In a medium-size bowl, mix all the ingredients for the mayonnaise and taste for seasoning. Add additional salt or pepper if needed. Cover and refrigerate until needed.

Prepare the chicken: Separate the meat from the bones and remove the skin, if desired. Slice the chicken into thin strips and set aside.

In a small frying pan, melt the butter over moderate heat. Add the almonds and sauté until golden brown, about 4–5 minutes. Drain on paper towels and set aside.

Assemble the salad: In a large bowl, mix the chicken slices with three-quarters of the mayonnaise, adding more mayonnaise if the salad seems dry. Gently stir in the sautéed almonds and half of the grapes.

Place the salad on a large serving plate and surround with the watercress and remaining grapes. Serve with buttered toast and any remaining mayonnaise on the side. *Serves 4.*

6

Oriental Sauces

Soy Sauce Tamari, Hoisin Sauce, Oyster Sauce, Satay Sauce

ALTHOUGH CHINESE CUISINE differs greatly from Japanese, just as Thai does from Indonesian, there is one common characteristic that links all Oriental cuisines. It is the idea of contrasting and balancing tastes and textures – what the Chinese call *yin* and *yang*. This philosophy permeates all facets of Eastern culture and in Oriental cooking it's expressed in many ways – hot and sour, crisp and gelatinous, sweet and sour.

Oriental sauces are also created with this philosophy in mind. A sweet-and-sour plum sauce provides flavour and contrast to a garlicky prawn dish. The pungent taste of Chinese oyster sauce highlights the almost bland flavour of stir-fried lettuce. A smooth, citrus-flavoured soy sauce adds sharp contrast to Japanese-style boiled beef with vegetables.

Oriental sauces are used to accentuate the natural flavours of food, not to conceal or overwhelm them. And they are an essential part of a wide variety of Oriental dishes. Some of these sauces are well known to Western cooks; others are exotic and unfamiliar. Experiment with all of them. You'll find that they add an incredibly good flavour to both Eastern and Western dishes.

ORIENTAL SAUCE SURVEY

Fish Sauce: South East Asia

Two and a half thousand years ago the Chinese created a dark, salty sauce made of fermented fish. Years later, soybeans were

103

substituted for fish. While soy sauce went on to become the most widely used condiment in China and Japan, fish sauce remains a basic flavouring ingredient throughout South East Asia. It is known by several names, including *patis, nuoc nam, nam pla* and *sauce de poisson.*

Fish sauce is made from fresh anchovies, fish or shrimp layered with salt in huge wooden barrels. This mixture is allowed to ferment for up to eight months. The very best fish sauce, which is the first taken from the barrel, is clear and light brown in colour. It's used, almost exclusively, as a table condiment and is the most expensive type of fish sauce. Lower quality (and less expensive) fish sauces come from the bottom of the barrel; these thicker, heavier sauces are used primarily for cooking.

TASTING NOTES:

Fish sauce is rather an acquired taste. A friend of mine once described its flavour as being like 'rotten anchovies turned into liquid.' I wouldn't go that far. Used in moderation, fish sauce provides a subtle, salty fish flavour to soups, stews and marinades. It is frequently used as a seafood dipping sauce (see recipe on page 117). It's also good with Oriental noodle dishes and grilled seafood shish kebab. Fish sauce can be used the same way as soy sauce, but remember that it has a very strong flavour – a little bit goes a long way.

Hoisin **Sauce: Chinese (Chinese Barbecue or Peking Sauce)**

It is mahogany coloured, has a thick consistency and a slightly sweet, spicy, almost smoky flavour. Made from mashed and fermented soybeans, garlic, chilli peppers, spices and flour, *hoisin* sauce has a unique way of highlighting the natural flavours in food, without drowning them out of existence.

Hoisin sauce is sometimes used in the preparation of Chinese dishes, but it is most often served as a condiment and dipping sauce. It is also called Chinese barbecue sauce because of the way it complements barbecued meats and poultry. *Hoisin* sauce also goes by the name Peking sauce, because it is the traditional condiment served with Peking duck, one of the most sophisticated and spectacular of all Chinese dishes.

Anyone who has ever had the pleasure of eating suckling pig in a really fine Chinese restaurant knows about the capabilities of *hoisin* sauce. Traditionally, the whole, freshly cooked pig is brought to the table for everyone to admire. Then the waiter brings the pig back into the kitchen where the chef skilfully slices the crisp, crackling skin into small squares and then reassembles them back onto the pig's flesh. The first course consists of the crisp pig skin, served with small squares of steamed bread, slivers of fresh spring onion and a bowl of *hoisin* sauce. (The *hoisin* helps to 'cut' the greasiness of the pig skin.) A 'sandwich' is prepared in which the pig skin, spring onion and a generous dab of *hoisin* sauce are placed between the hot bread. It is an unforgettable taste sensation.

TASTING NOTES:
Hoisin sauce can be used in marinades (it's particularly good with spare-ribs) and as a dipping sauce for meats and fish. It's delicious served with shellfish, duck and chicken. A touch of sesame oil mixed into the *hoisin* sauce adds a really nice flavour; serve it with Peking pancakes or barbecued duck or chicken.

Lemon Sauce: Chinese

Made from lemons, sugar and water, this is a thick, jamlike sauce. Because of its tart, sweet flavour, the Chinese like to serve it as a condiment with duck and chicken. Diluted with a bit of cold water, it makes a great dipping sauce for slightly cooked, still-crisp vegetables. It can also be spread on toast like lemon jam.

Oyster Sauce: Chinese

The small fishing village at Lau Fah Shan on the South China Sea in Hong Kong is famous for its oysters. Walking through the narrow, open-air seafood market, you see baskets of fresh shellfish being hauled in from the beach. These oysters are not the familiar variety found in American waters, *Ostrea edulis*, but a larger species, *Cassotred gigas*. They are about 7.5–10 cm/3–4 in long, almost the size of a child's shoe. At Lau Fah Shan, young boys spend their entire days, with chisels and long spikes in hand, opening the enormous shells. These oysters are never eaten raw; they are primarily used to make the prized Cantonese condiment, oyster sauce.

This thick, velvety brown sauce is made from dried oysters that are pounded with soy sauce, salt and other seasonings and then fermented in porcelain crocks for several years; the best oyster sauces are allowed to ferment for up to seven or eight years.

TASTING NOTES:

You don't have to be mad about oysters to like oyster sauce. It doesn't taste fishy. It is rich, pungent and somewhat salty, intensifying the natural flavours of food without imposing a strong taste of its own.

When buying oyster sauce, look for a relatively thin sauce with a light-brown colour. If the sauce is dark brown, very thick or has a foamy substance on the top of the jar, it is not of good quality. Unfortunately, FDA food regulations in the United States demand that extra salt be added to preserve the oyster sauce that is imported from Hong Kong and China. As a result, most of the oyster sauce you find in American food shops is terribly salty. The best way to use oyster sauce is diluted with a drop of water; it cuts the salt and gives the sauce a thinner, more desirable consistency.

Oyster sauce is frequently used to flavour and thicken other sauces, but its primary use is as a condiment. My favourite way to use oyster sauce is drizzled over steamed or stir-fried vegetables. A simple plate of steamed spinach can be transformed into a rich, exotic dish with just a touch of oyster sauce on top. Use it with Chinese broccoli, mustard greens, *bok choy* (Chinese cabbage) or steamed lettuce. Oyster sauce also makes a good dipping sauce for dumplings, seafood, grilled beef, shish kebab and chicken. It is also a terrific marinade ingredient for steaks, chops and chicken.

Plum (or Duck) Sauce: Chinese

Plum sauce is that sweet, chutney-like goo that comes in those clear little plastic packets you often find in Chinese restaurants. Nine times out of ten, it's pretty dismal stuff. Most commercially made brands of plum sauce are loaded with sugar (it's usually the main ingredient) and preservatives. There are, however, some brands that are really good.

TASTING NOTES:

Plum sauce is made from plums, apricots, chilli peppers, garlic, vinegar and sugar; sometimes ginger or sweet potatoes are added, too. It is traditionally served with Chinese duck (which is where it gets its nickname from), but it also makes a delicious dipping sauce for chicken, prawns, spring rolls and steamed or fried dumplings. Plum sauce can also be used as a glaze for roast pork, spare-ribs, chicken and roast meats.

Satay Sauce: Indonesian and Chinese

Satay, or barbecue, is the national dish of Indonesia. Each island prepares its *satay* differently, and for each variation there is a different type of *satay* sauce. The traditional sauce is a rich, thick blend of ground peanuts, tamarind, chillies, garlic, coconut and shrimp paste. (See page 116 for a peanut and chilli *satay* sauce recipe.)

TASTING NOTES:
Satay sauce is served with pork, chicken or beef barbecue. It also makes a delicious topping for cold Chinese noodles or a spicy dip for shish kebab, grilled prawns or raw vegetables.

Soy Sauces: Chinese and Japanese

Soy sauce is believed to be one of the oldest condiments in the world. The story goes that some 2,500 years ago the Chinese created a fermented fish and meat sauce they called *chiang*. Years later, as Buddhism became increasingly popular, the Chinese substituted soybeans for fish and meat so that they could continue to use the sauce as part of their new vegetarian diet.

Soy sauce made its way to Japan in the early part of the sixth century. The Japanese took an immediate liking to the sauce but found that it overpowered the natural flavours of their food. So they experimented with the basic recipe of soybeans, wheat, salt and water. By adding a higher proportion of wheat and allowing the sauce to ferment over a long period of time, the Japanese created a lighter, more delicate version of soy sauce. By the fifteenth century, soy sauce became so popular in Japan that the Japanese began commercially producing their own type of soy sauce called *shoyu*.

We definitely don't associate soy sauce with European cuisine, but in the seventeenth century Dutch traders exported jugs of the Oriental sauce from Nagasaki to Europe. Initially, it was considered an exotic seasoning that only the elite could afford. King Louis XIV of France was so taken by its flavour that he served it at his most elaborate court banquets.

Soy sauce was first exported to the United States in the late eighteenth century when Japanese workers living there became homesick for it. Needless to say, it became very popular with Americans as well.

The first stage in making traditional, naturally brewed soy sauce is called *koji* – a Japanese word meaning 'bloom of mould'. Essentially, soybeans and wheat are mixed with a starter yeast called Aspergillus. The mixture is placed into large perforated vats where it matures for about three days.

In the second step, a brine or water and salt solution is added, and the mixture is transferred to deep fermentation tanks where it is kept for anything from six months to three years. This is the most crucial stage in making soy sauce. As the mixture ages, the sauce develops its sweet, salty, tart flavour and its rich aroma and deep dark-brown colour.

The final step involves pressing the raw soy sauce from the soy 'cake' (which consists of the fermented soybean and wheat hulls). The sauce is then refined and pasteurised before being bottled.

As with almost everything else these days, there is also a high-tech, synthetic method for making soy sauce that allows the whole process to take place in about three to four days. Instead of allowing the sauce to age and develop flavour naturally, the soybeans are boiled with hydrochloric acid in order to induce fermentation. Salt is then added together with corn syrup for sweetness and caramel for colour. Many of these synthetically produced soy sauces are made in the United States and labelled under Chinese-sounding brand names. They are generally a little cheaper than naturally brewed soy sauces but they have a definitely artificial flavour.

The best way to tell the difference between a bottle of naturally brewed and synthetic soy sauce is to read the label. Look for the words 'naturally brewed'. This is your guarantee that the traditional, natural process has been used. Next, read the ingredients listed on the label. A really good soy sauce is made only from soybeans, wheat (which is sometimes listed as flour), salt and water. Stay away from brands that contain additives or sweeteners. Another test is to take a bottle of soy sauce and shake it vigorously until bubbles form on the top. If the soy sauce has been naturally fermented, it will form a thick, foamy head, similar to beer, that will take a few seconds to subside.

There are dozens of varieties of soy sauce sold in the United States, the majority of which come from China, Hong Kong and Japan. Most people think they all taste pretty much the same, but there is a big difference between light and dark soy and Japanese and Chinese soy sauce. Each sauce has its own distinct flavour, colour, aroma and consistency and each one is meant to be used differently. What follows is a brief description of the most common types of soy sauce, and hints on how and when they should be used.

Chinese Soy Sauce

Chinese soy sauce tends to have a stronger, saltier flavour than Japanese soy sauce. Because Chinese soy sauces contains less wheat than the Japanese sauces, they also tend to have a more pronounced soy flavour.

Throughout China it's not uncommon to find dozens of different varieties of soy sauce. In the United States, however, there are essentially three basic types of soy sauce. They are as follows:

Light (or Pale or Thin) Soy Sauce: Light soy sauce is taken from the top of the fermentation tanks while the heavier, darker sauces come from the bottom. This is the most versatile type of Chinese soy sauce. It is used primarily as a table condiment and dipping sauce but can also be used for cooking when you want a light soy flavour.

Black (or Dark or Thick) Soy Sauce: The addition of caramel gives this soy sauce its rich colour, thick consistency and sweet flavour. Although it is sometimes served as a table condiment, dark soy sauce is primarily used for cooking, particularly with stir-fried foods.

Use dark soy sauce to add flavour to soups, stews, casseroles and roasts. It's also delicious in marinades for beef, pork, chicken and spare-ribs.

Heavy (or Double Black) Soy Sauce: This is the least popular variety of Chinese soy sauce, probably because the addition of molasses makes it rather heavy and sweet. It is used, almost exclusively, in cooking and is prized in China for its rich dark colour. Use sparingly; heavy soy sauce can easily overpower delicately flavoured foods.

TASTING NOTES:

- Sprinkle light Chinese soy sauce over cold tofu with sesame seeds and flakes of dried bonito (fish).
- Light Chinese soy sauce has a slightly sweet flavour that goes particularly well with prawns. Try stir-frying prawns, pea pods, peanuts and thinly sliced spring onions in a mixture of peanut oil and sesame oil. Add a liberal dash of soy sauce and serve.
- Mix soy sauce with garlic and ginger and serve as a dipping sauce for grilled chicken, *dim sum*, or fried dumplings.
- Try stir-frying in butter and add a touch of light soy at the last minute. It makes a dark-brown buttery sauce that complements the sweet flavour of the peas.

- Add a dash of soy sauce to vinaigrettes and serve with a green salad.
- Serve black Chinese soy sauce with grilled pork chops and seafood shish kebab.

Japanese Soy Sauce *(Shoyu)*

On the whole, Japanese soy sauces are more delicate, less salty and a bit sweeter than the Chinese variety. After experimenting for hundreds of years, the Japanese discovered that by adding equal quantities of soybeans and wheat, a sweeter soy sauce resulted. Many people believe that the additional wheat also gives the sauce a milder, more well-rounded flavour.

TASTING NOTES:

Japanese soy sauce can be used for cooking or as a table condiment. It's delicious with grilled fish, noodles and steamed vegetables. Add it to stews, soups and casseroles or use as a dipping sauce. Mixed with hot peppers and sesame seeds, it makes a great dipping sauce for grilled steak or prawns. Because soy sauce contains enzymes that tenderise foods, it is an especially good ingredient for marinades.

Soy sauce mixed with a touch of *wasabi* (green Japanese horseradish root) is the traditional dipping sauce for *sushi* and *sashimi*. According to Kinjirō Ōmae and Yuzuru Tachibana in *The Book of Sushi*, 'Because of the way it masks the rawness of fresh uncooked fish and harmonises with such other ingredients as seaweed, soy sauce is indispensable to *sushi*. Indeed, it could be said that without soy sauce, *sushi* would probably never have reached its present state of development.'

Tamari: **Japanese-American**

Tamari and soy sauce look, taste and smell almost identical. But, unlike soy sauce, *tamari* has always been sold as a 'health food' product 'free from preservatives and additives'. The truth is *tamari* is practically the same thing as naturally brewed soy sauce. The major difference is that *tamari* contains very little, if any, wheat. (Most soy sauces contain 30–50 per cent wheat; *tamari* generally has only 10 per cent wheat.) Because there is less wheat, *tamari* tends to have a full (some call it strong) soy flavour.

TASTING NOTES:
Use *tamari* as you would a full-flavour soy sauce. It makes a delicious salad dressing mixed with lemon juice and a light olive (or pure peanut) oil.

Goma: **Japanese**

This thick, sesame-seed-flavoured soy sauce is traditionally served as a condiment with *shabu-shabu*, the Japanese equivalent of beef fondue. It is made from toasted and ground sesame seeds mixed with Japanese soy sauce, *dashi* (a light, Japanese, kelp-flavoured broth) and sugar.

TASTING NOTES:
Goma makes a fantastic dipping sauce for grilled chicken, raw vegetables, fish or steak. Mix in a teaspoon of sesame oil and serve it with a cold tofu salad or grilled prawns.

Ketjap Manis or *Ketjap Benteng:* **Indonesian**

This thick, sweet, almost syrupy Indonesian soy sauce is made with the addition of sugar, molasses and assorted spices. The Indonesian word *ketjap* means 'a sauce added to food for extra flavour'. Some etymologists believe this is the root of our word for 'ketchup'; see page 89 for more.

TASTING NOTES:
Ketjap Manis is served with a wide variety of Indonesian dishes and is always present at the traditional Indonesian banquet called *rijsttafel*. It's particularly good served with *satay* (Indonesian barbecue), grilled fish, chicken or steamed vegetables.

Mushroom Soy Sauce: Chinese

Mushroom soy sauce is a naturally fermented Chinese soy sauce made with the addition of mushrooms. The mushrooms are added towards the end of the fermentation process and they give this sauce a rich, earthy flavour.

TASTING NOTES:
Use mushroom soy sauce for stir-frying vegetables, meats, poultry and fish. Sprinkle it over rice and noodle dishes and into soups and stews. Its flavour can quickly become addictive.

Ponzu Sauce: Japanese

This delicious, citrus-flavoured soy sauce is a traditional accompaniment to *shabu-shabu*, the Japanese version of fondue. *Ponzu* sauce and *goma* (see page 111) are served side by side with the *shabu-shabu* dish.

Ponzu sauce is a light Japanese soy sauce flavoured with rice vinegar, lemon and lime juice. You can make your own simply by mixing 120 ml/4 fl oz lemon juice, 120 ml/4 fl oz lime juice with 350 ml/12 fl oz Japanese soy sauce and 5 tablespoons Japanese rice vinegar. Add *mirin* (a sweet Japanese rice wine) to taste.

TASTING NOTES:
Serve *ponzu* sauce with *shabu-shabu* or over a crisp vegetable salad, grilled fish or chicken. It's wonderful sprinkled over a cold seafood and avocado salad.

Tentsuyu Sauce: Japanese

This flavoured soy sauce is a traditional accompaniment to tempura (batter-fried fish and vegetables). There are a number of brands of prepared *tentsuyu* on the market; unfortunately, most of them are filled with MSG and other preservatives. You can make your own simply by heating up 120 ml/4 fl oz *dashi* (a light Japanese stock made from kelp and seaweed) or water with 1½ tablespoons light Japanese soy sauce and 1½ tablespoons *mirin* (a sweet Japanese rice wine); add sugar to taste. It's also nice to add a touch of grated ginger to the sauce. Serve warm as a dipping sauce with assorted tempura or with Japanese noodle dishes, grilled chicken or fish.

Teriyaki **Sauce: Japanese**

Teriyaki literally means 'glaze-grill', which refers to a method of cooking meats, fish and poultry that originated in Japan centuries ago. The original *teriyaki* sauce was made simply of soy sauce and *mirin* (a sweet Japanese rice wine) with a touch of sugar. It was used primarily to marinate and baste grilled fish.

When the Japanese began emigrating to Hawaii, they altered the sauce by adding local seasonings – fresh ginger, brown sugar and green onions. Many of the commercially produced *teriyaki* sauces are based on this Hawaiian recipe.

TASTING NOTES:
Although *teriyaki* sauce is still used as a marinade ingredient or as a basting (or glazing) sauce, it also makes an excellent condiment. Sprinkle it over stir-fried vegetables, grilled chicken or fish and salads. It's particularly delicious as a dipping sauce for tempura or fried chicken. It's easy to make your own *teriyaki* sauce; see page 115 for a recipe.

Sweet-and-Sour Sauce: Chinese-American

The contrast of sweet and sour flavours is an ancient Chinese culinary tradition. There are endless variations of sweet-and-sour sauce, all based on the combination of sugar, vinegar and fruit. Unfortunately, most Americans' idea of sweet-and-sour sauce is that pinkish-red, gooey sweet stuff that is slopped onto chicken and fish in almost every Chinese restaurant in America. Capitalising on America's familiarity with sweet-and-sour sauce, many companies are now marketing a Westernised version of Chinese plum sauce, which they call 'sweet-and-sour sauce'.

TASTING NOTES:
These sauces can be used for dipping fried prawns, chicken or fish, or served as a condiment with stir-fried beef, spring rolls and dumplings. Sweet-and-sour sauce makes a delicious glaze for roast ham and spare-ribs.

Tonkatsu **Sauce: Japanese**

This is a dark, spicy sauce that is traditionally served with *tonkatsu* – Japanese-style fried pork cutlet. Made from tomatoes, apples, carrots and onions, *tonkatsu* sauce is like a thick, spicy Japanese version of ketchup.

TASTING NOTES:
Serve *tonkatsu* sauce with fried pork, chicken or fish. It's also delicious on hamburgers with thinly sliced spring onions.

MAKING YOUR OWN ORIENTAL SAUCES

Home-made Flavoured Soy Sauce

There are an amazing number of flavoured soy sauces available in Oriental and speciality food shops these days. But a quick look at the list of ingredients reveals that all there is to most of them is soy sauce mixed with one or two flavouring ingredients, lots of sugar and loads of preservatives. What's the point?

Making flavoured soy sauce at home is simple and inexpensive. The key is to use your imagination. It's amazing how easily soy sauce mingles with other flavours. *The basic 'recipe' for making flavoured soy sauce is: 120 ml/4 fl oz soy sauce mixed with 2–3 tablespoons of flavouring ingredients.* There's usually no need to add sugar or salt; the soy sauce is already sweet and salty.

Home-made flavoured soy sauce makes a wonderful gift. Pour the soy sauce out of its bottle and mix with the flavourings. Then, funnel the sauce back into the bottle and place your own label describing the sauce over the one already on the bottle. You can also place a piece of decorative fabric and ribbon over the cap. Be sure to keep these flavoured soy sauces refrigerated.

Listed below are a few of my favourite combinations. Use them as dipping sauces with *sushi* and *sashimi*, grilled prawns, dumplings, Chinese stir-fries, and shish kebab. They are also delicious sprinkled over grilled meats, poultry and fish and as a base for salad dressing.

114

Favourite Flavoured-Soy-Sauce Combinations

- Soy sauce mixed with *wasabi* (ground Japanese horseradish)
- Soy sauce with lemon and lime juice and thinly sliced spring onions
- Chilli-pepper-and-spring onion-flavoured soy sauce
- Orange-flavoured soy sauce (with fresh orange juice and grated orange rind)
- Soy sauce flavoured with sesame paste and sesame oil
- Hot Chinese-mustard-flavoured soy sauce
- Soy sauce with Japanese rice vinegar, minced fresh ginger and spring onions
- Soy sauce with minced pickled plums
- Soy sauce with grated ginger, garlic and sesame oil
- Soy sauce with grated *daikon* (Japanese radish)
- Soy sauce with dry Chinese mustard and red wine vinegar
- Soy sauce with hot chilli oil and chopped roasted peanuts

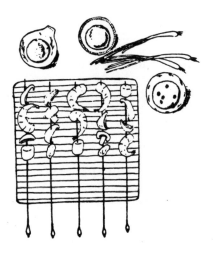

Home-made *Teriyaki* Sauce

Although there are a few good commercially produced brands of *teriyaki* sauce, most of them are filled with sugar and preservatives. This is a simple, not-too-sweet recipe for making your own. It will keep in the refrigerator for several weeks.

Use as a dipping sauce for raw vegetables and fried foods, or spoon over rice and noodle dishes. The sauce is also delicious as a marinade for meat, chicken or fish, and as a glaze for *teriyaki*.

150 ml/¼ pint light Japanese soy sauce
120 ml/4 fl oz *mirin* (sweet Japanese rice wine)
1½ teaspoons rice vinegar
1½ teaspoons brown sugar
2 teaspoons finely minced fresh ginger
2 cloves minced garlic

In a medium bowl, mix all the ingredients and leave, covered, for about 2 hours. You can either serve the sauce as is, or strain out the bits of ginger and garlic. Keep refrigerated. *Makes about 250 ml/8 fl oz.*

Peanut and Chilli *Satay* Sauce

This thick, spicy *satay* sauce can be served with barbecued pork, chicken or beef. It also makes a delicious dip for raw vegetables, or a topping for cold Chinese noodles.

120 g/4½ oz crunchy peanut butter
3 thinly sliced fresh chilli peppers, with seeds
1 large clove minced garlic
1 tablespoon sugar
½ teaspoon cayenne pepper
2½ tablespoons lime juice
2½ tablespoons Chinese dark soy sauce
1½ tablespoons peanut oil
2 tablespoons water

Mix together the peanut butter, chillies, garlic, sugar and cayenne pepper. Stir in the lime juice, soy sauce, oil and water until smooth. Let the *satay* stand at room temperature for 30 minutes before serving. *Makes about 120 ml/4 fl oz.*

Ginger-and-Garlic-Flavoured Soy Sauce with Radishes

Thinly sliced radishes mixed with soy sauce, rice vinegar, ginger and garlic create this unusual condiment. You can use this as a dipping sauce with fried fish, chicken or tempura. It's also delicious spooned over steamed rice, stir-fried vegetables, salads, grilled fish, or even a steak. Don't make this sauce too far in advance because the radishes will lose their crunchy texture after about 24 hours.

20 radishes, very thinly sliced
1 tablespoon minced fresh ginger
2 cloves garlic, minced
5 tablespoons light soy sauce
5 tablespoons rice vinegar
1 tablespoon sesame oil
3 tablespoons *mirin* (sweet Japanese rice wine)

Place the radishes in a large bowl and mix in the remaining ingredients. Cover and place in the refrigerator; marinate for 2–4 hours and serve cold. *Makes about 250 ml/8 fl oz.*

Hot and Spicy Dipping Sauce

This sauce goes well with all sorts of rice and noodle dishes, but it is outrageously good with fried chicken. To make a Chinese-style fried chicken, heat about 1 litre/1¾ pints pure Chinese peanut oil in a wok along with a tablespoon of sesame oil and a few slivers of fresh garlic and ginger. Let the oil get very hot. Lightly flour chicken pieces and deep-fry until crisp and completely cooked, about 20–25 minutes. Drain on paper towels and serve with this pungent sauce.

5 tablespoons light Chinese soy sauce
1½ tablespoons finely minced fresh ginger
1 teaspoon thinly sliced fresh chilli pepper, red or green
1 tablespoon Oriental sesame oil

Mix all the ingredients in a small saucepan and heat over a moderately low heat for about 5 minutes. Taste for seasoning; if the sauce is too spicy, add additional soy sauce. Serve warm. *Makes about 120 ml/4 fl oz.*

Vietnamese Sweet-and-Sour Fish Sauce

Serve this sweet-and-sour dipping sauce with fried noodles, fish or chicken. Covered, it will keep in the refrigerator for several weeks.

> 4 tablespoons fish sauce, see page 103
> 120 ml/4 fl oz cold water
> 2 tablespoons fresh lime juice
> 2 tablespoons sugar
> ½ teaspoon chopped fresh hot-red chilli pepper or 1 small dried red pepper, crumbled
> 1 clove minced garlic

In a small bowl, whisk together all the ingredients until the sugar is dissolved. Serve at room temperature. *Makes about 250 ml/8 fl oz.*

COOKING WITH ORIENTAL SAUCES

Soy and Tahini Dressing

This dressing is delicious on a salad made of romaine, Boston lettuce and watercress. It's also good on a cold steamed vegetable salad.

> 1 teaspoon Dijon mustard
> 1 teaspoon sesame tahini
> pinch of freshly grated black pepper
> 2½ teaspoons light Chinese or Japanese soy sauce
> 1 teaspoon lemon juice

1½ teaspoons sesame oil
3 tablespoons red wine vinegar, or rice vinegar
4 teaspoons olive oil, preferably virgin or extra virgin

In a large salad bowl, stir together the mustard, sesame tahini and pepper to form a smooth paste. Add the remaining ingredients in the order listed and stir until smooth. *Makes about 5 tablespoons.*

Stir-Fried French Beans with Sausage and Oyster Sauce

This dish takes only a few minutes to cook, so all your ingredients should be pre-chopped and ready to go.

1 tablespoon peanut oil
1 tablespoon sesame oil
2 cloves minced garlic
1 small minced shallot
1 tablespoon minced fresh ginger
2 pork sausages, thinly sliced
450 g/1 lb French beans, cut on the diagonal into
4 cm/1½ in long pieces
2½ tablespoons dark Chinese soy sauce
2 tablespoons water
oyster sauce

Heat a wok or a large frying pan over a high heat until hot, about 2–3 minutes. Add the oils and heat until almost to the smoking point. Add the garlic, shallot and ginger and cook for about 5 seconds, or until they begin to turn golden brown. Add the sausages and cook for about 2–4 minutes, or until brown. Remove the sausages and seasonings with a slotted spoon and reserve on a paper towel.

Add the beans to the hot wok and cook 2–3 minutes, or until crisp and slightly brown. Add the sausages and seasonings with the soy sauce and the water. Allow the mixture to boil for a minute or until slightly thickened and remove from the heat. Place on a serving dish and drizzle the beans with oyster sauce. *Serves 2 as a main course and 4 as a side dish.*

Grilled Haddock with *Tamari,* Ginger and Garlic

This is a delicious and simple way to cook fresh haddock. The *tamari,* together with the ginger and garlic, creates a dark, rich glaze for the fish fillet.

1 kg/2 lb haddock fillets
1½ tablespoons minced fresh ginger
2 cloves minced garlic
120 ml/4 fl oz *tamari,* Chinese or Japanese soy sauce or *teriyaki* sauce
25 g/1 oz butter, cut into small pieces

Preheat the grill. Lightly oil a baking sheet or grill pan and place the fish in the centre. Insert the ginger and garlic into the fish's flesh and pour the soy sauce over the top. Dot with the butter and place under the grill for about 10 minutes, or until the fish turns golden brown and flakes when tested with a fork. *Serves 4–6.*

Steak Marinated in Sweet Japanese Soy Sauce

You can use this pungent marinade with steak (about 750 g/1½ lb) or double the recipe and use with chicken (about 1.5 kg/3 lb cut into serving pieces). The meat marinates for about 45 minutes (the soy sauce will help to tenderise the meat); it is then grilled or barbecued and the marinade is boiled and used as a sauce.

175 ml/6 fl oz Japanese soy sauce
120 ml/4 fl oz *mirin* (sweet Japanese rice wine)
2 tablespoons minced fresh ginger
2 cloves minced garlic
1 tablespoon frozen orange juice concentrate
1 tablespoon home-made Chinese hot chilli oil (see recipe on page 59), or sesame oil
1 tablespoon honey
750 g/1½ lb sirloin steak
1 tablespoon cornflour

In a large bowl, whisk together all the ingredients, except the cornflour. Place the meat or chicken into the mixture and toss to coat thoroughly. Leave to marinate at room temperature for about 45 minutes to an hour.

Preheat the grill or barbecue. Remove the meat (or chicken) from the marinade and grill or barbecue the meat until cooked.

Meanwhile, place the marinade in a small saucepan and whisk in the cornflour, if desired. Bring the marinade to the boil over a high heat, reduce the heat, and allow to simmer for 2–4 minutes, or until slightly thickened.

Spoon a few tablespoons of the sauce over the grilled meat or chicken and serve the remaining sauce on the side. *Makes about 350 ml/12 fl oz of marinade.*

Chicken in Mushroom Soy Sauce, Vinegar and Garlic Sauce

This dish is based on *adobong*, the national dish of the Philippines. The chicken is marinated in soy sauce, vinegar and garlic and then gently simmered. The chicken is then grilled, while the marinade is reduced into a thick, rich sweet-and-sour sauce. It's a lot simpler than it sounds and delicious served with white rice and a watercress and orange salad.

1.5 kg/3 lb chicken, cut into serving pieces
250 ml/8 fl oz apple cider vinegar
175 ml/6 fl oz soy sauce, preferably mushroom soy
5 cloves garlic, minced
8 peppercorns
2 bay leaves
1½ tablespoons brown sugar (optional)

Place the chicken in a large casserole or saucepan and cover with the remaining ingredients; toss well to thoroughly coat the chicken pieces. Leave to marinate at room temperature for at least 1½ hours.

Over a moderately high heat, simmer the chicken until it is tender but not completely cooked, about 15 minutes. Preheat the grill. Remove the chicken from the sauce and place on a grill rack. Grill for about 10 minutes, or until the chicken is crisp, brown and cooked (when pierced with a fork or knife, the juices should be yellow and not pink).

Meanwhile, let the sauce boil over a high heat, skimming off any fat that comes to the surface. Allow to boil until it is thickened and reduced by half, about 10 minutes. Strain the reduced sauce over the chicken and serve. *Serves 3–4.*

7

Relishes, Pickles and Savoury Jellies

LATE SEPTEMBER. The days are often still warm and summery; the nights are beginning to turn cool, almost cold. The fruit trees and garden are in all their glory, but the first frost threatens. Out come the old family recipes, the preserving jars and lids. The peaches, tomatoes, corn, onions, peppers, beans and herbs are picked and an entire day – preferably a rainy one – is put aside for preserving.

Generation after generation of American cooks have gone through this ritual. Kitchens fill with the pungent scent of vinegar, herbs and spices as the last summer produce is sliced, chopped, diced and mixed into dozens of varieties of relishes, pickles and savoury jellies.

The jars are filled, tightly sealed and then placed in the pantry. Months later, when most of the country is covered with a foot of snow, the relishes, pickles and jellies packed inside these jars fill us with the tastes, smells and memories of summer.

RELISHES

In early American cooking, relishes were one of the favourite ways to preserve surplus fruits and garden vegetables. Everything from onions, peppers, cabbage and corn to cranberries, pears, peaches and apples were used.

The recipes varied from region to region, and kitchen to kitchen, but the essential idea was the same: to chop fresh fruits and vegetables, mix them with a spiced vinegar and let them 'pickle' for several months. The appeal of these relishes was that they provided 'fresh' food during the winter months and they masked the flavour of meat, which was not always of top quality.

For years the only relishes available in the United States were the home-made ones that lined the shelves in every family's pantry or 'preserve closet'. Cooks took great pride in serving a variety of home-made relishes at special meals and celebrations.

In the late 1800s commercial relishes began to appear. Mr Henry Heinz bottled a sweet pepper relish and, like his other new product, tomato ketchup, it became a popular way of enlivening the flavour of meats, poultry and fish.

At the time, commercially made relish was considered a great new convenience, but over the years convenience seems to have won out over quality. And so now what passes for relish is nothing more than sugar and corn syrup mixed with overcooked cucumbers and peppers. You know what I mean – the bright green, sweet, gelatinous stuff that's served with hot dogs and hamburgers in food bars everywhere.

Recently some commercially made relishes have appeared on the market that are reminiscent of the home-made variety. In larger supermarkets and speciality food shops, you can now find a wide assortment of relishes that have the fresh taste and texture of the fruits, vegetables, spices and herbs that went into making them.

The very best relishes, however, are still the ones that you make at home. Relish is incredibly easy to make; see pages 130–5 for some delicious recipes.

TASTING NOTES:
- Pepper relish is the classic accompaniment to hot dogs and hamburgers. It also goes well with sausages and barbecued meats.
- Relishes go particularly well with spicy foods; try serving an assortment of fresh relishes with curries or meats, chicken and fish that have been grilled in a spicy pepper sauce.
- Serve a home-made pepper relish as a dipping sauce for grilled prawns, steamed crab or deep-fried, batter-coated vegetables.
- Add a teaspoon of onion, corn or cranberry relish to a sharp Cheddar cheese sandwich.
- Turkey, egg and chicken salads take on a whole new flavour when relish is added. One of my favourite recipes is: 300 g/11 oz of thinly sliced chicken or turkey mixed with about 120 ml/4 fl oz home-made mayonnaise (see recipe on page 97), a tablespoon of Dijon mustard and a tablespoon of red wine vinegar. Add about 3 tablespoons of Five Pepper Relish (see my recipe on page 130), and add 25 g/1 oz chopped walnuts and raisins. Serve with watercress and toasted pumpernickel bread.
- Spread a tablespoon of piccalilli on a sliced turkey, duck or chicken sandwich.
- Serve a corn, onion or cucumber relish with fried chicken.
- Serve chowchow with lamb curry or roast ham.
- Try a spicy tomato relish on a hamburger or grilled flank steak.
- Add a tablespoon of relish to an avocado and beetroot salad.

PICKLES

When I think of pickles I immediately flash to childhood scenes at our neighbourhood deli. I can see the large wooden barrels sitting on the sawdust-strewn floor. Inside those barrels were dill, sour and half-sour pickles floating in a spicy vinegar mixture flavoured with mustard seeds, peppercorns and bay leaves. Their intense, pungent scent overwhelmed the deli. At least twice a week, I'd go there and buy two huge, crisp dill pickles, a grilled hot dog with mustard and sauerkraut and a cold cream soda. To me, that was heaven.

You can't buy pickles like that in a jar. Commercially made dill, sour and half-sours can't even come close to the flavour of deli pickles. But, I'm happy to say, you can still find delicious, home-made cucumber pickles at some delis.

I could write an entire book on pickles. They are made in practically every country in the world in endless variations. Here I've dealt with just a few, more unusual pickles that are traditionally served as condiments – wonderful treats like pickled onions and walnuts from England, pickled ginger from Japan, pickled okra from the American South, pickled gherkins from France, and more.

TASTING NOTES:
- Serve a selection of pickles as part of an antipasto salad.
- Chop pickles into chicken, turkey, duck and egg salads.
- Serve pickles with hot dogs, hamburgers and sandwiches.
- Finely chop a few pieces of pickled watermelon rind and serve on a barbecued pork sandwich on a thick roll.
- Pickles go well with cold curry salad, particularly a very hot and spicy chicken or beef curry.
- Pickled black walnuts are a traditional English accompaniment to roast beef, but they also go well with roast lamb, duck and pork.
- Finely chop French *cornichons* and mix into a vinaigrette with a few finely chopped pimentos. Serve as a dipping sauce for grilled prawns, poached salmon or grilled fish.
- Serve watermelon rind pickle and pickled onions at a picnic with fried chicken and herb biscuits.
- Thinly slice pickled onions and serve on a roast beef sandwich.
- Pickled Oriental radishes (see recipe on page 135) are delicious served with Japanese tempura and Oriental-style rice dishes.

Cornichons

Cornichons are very small pickled gherkin cucumbers. Throughout France – from the most chic Parisian restaurants to small, family-run country bistros – these crisp, tart pickles are the traditional accompaniment to pâtés and cold meat platters.

Cornichons are delicate pickles. They are delicious straight out of the jar, but they can also be served with cheeses, smoked meats and fish, roast chicken, cold poached salmon or fried fish. They add a wonderful crunchy texture and piquant flavour to vinaigrettes, mayonnaise, and tartare sauce (see recipe on page 99).

Other Pickles

Some of the very best pickles are the home-made ones sold at local country fairs and community barbecues. Look out for them; they are almost always made from old family recipes using the very best local vegetables, fruits and herbs.

SAVOURY JELLIES

Although I have been known to spread raspberry jelly on a cheese sandwich and jelly made from tiny, ripe strawberries on roast pork, sweet jellies are generally not served as condiments.

Savoury jellies – jellies flavoured with a variety of herbs, spices and chilli peppers – make delicious accompaniments to roast meats, poultry and fish.

Herb Jellies

Herb jellies have been popular in Europe since the Middle Ages. Simmering fresh garden herbs and apples into a home-made jelly was considered an art and a great delicacy. Recently, however, a number of English and American companies have started making jellies flavoured with rosemary, sage, basil, oregano, summer savory, lemon balm, parsley and rose geranium leaf.

Herb jellies have a wonderful fresh herb scent and a subtle, yet distinctive herb flavour.

TASTING NOTES:
- Herb jellies are most frequently served with meats – roast beef, lamb or pork or grilled lamb or pork chops.
- Serve herb jellies with roast chicken, duck and goose.
- Slice a ripe tomato in half, spread with a tablespoon of herb jelly on top and grill. Serve with roasts.
- Fill hot muffins and home-made biscuits with herb jelly.
- Heat herb jelly and serve as a dipping sauce for a vegetable kebab.
- Add herb jelly to steamed carrots, peas, beetroot or French beans.

- Whisk herb jellies into sauces and gravies.
- Heat herb jellies and use as a glaze for chicken, duck, lamb, ham or prawns.
- Spread herb jellies on buttered toast and top with thin slices of Cheddar cheese.
- Make a herb jelly omelette.
- Spread herb jellies on top of pancakes.

Pepper Jelly

The idea of simmering hot chilli peppers into a sweet, spicy jelly probably originated in the American south-west. In the last few years, however, hot pepper jelly has become popular across the United States.

Hot pepper jelly is made from hot chilli peppers, sweet green or red peppers, sugar, vinegar and pectin. The bright red or green colour of the jelly is not natural; a few drops of artificial colouring are added to most commercially made pepper jellies.

TASTING NOTES:
- The most popular way to serve pepper jelly is on biscuits with cream cheese.
- Hot pepper jelly is delicious served on just-baked, steaming-hot cornbread.
- Try it on a peanut butter, grilled cheese or cold lamb sandwich.
- Hot pepper jellies are great on steamed French beans, peas and thinly sliced carrots.
- Try heating the jelly and use it as a dip with dumplings, beef fondue, raw vegetables, fried chicken or grilled prawns.
- Mix a few tablespoons of hot pepper jelly with either soured cream or yogurt and serve as a dip with raw vegetables or taco chips.
- Try pepper jelly (instead of mustard) with a variety of grilled sausages.
- Instead of a traditional pepper relish, serve a hot dog with pepper jelly and sautéed onions.
- Mix pepper jellies into salad dressings.
- Serve pepper jellies with pâtés, cheeses and cold meats.
- Serve pepper jelly, like a mint sauce, with roasts.

MAKING YOUR OWN RELISHES, PICKLES AND SAVOURY JELLIES

Boiling Water Bath for Bottling Chutneys, Relishes and Pickles

For years I believed that bottling was a time-consuming and tedious process. Then, one August afternoon, I tried to bottle some leftover garden tomatoes and was amazed to see how easy it is. Bottling is a perfect and rewarding way to spend a rainy summer afternoon.

Keep in mind that this method is only good for foods with a high acid content; all the recipes in this book work with this method.

1. Wash jars and lids in hot, soapy water. Sterilise jars and lids in boiling water for 15 minutes. Remove with tongs and invert on a clean tea towel or on paper towels to dry.
2. Fill a preserving pan with water, or a pot large enough for the jars to be completely immersed and fully surrounded by boiling water. Make sure the pan has a rack on the bottom so the jars won't touch the bottom. (If you don't have a rack, simply wrap the jars in clean tea or dish towels. The jars should not touch each other while being processed.) Bring the water to a rolling boil.
3. Fill the sterilised jars with hot chutney, relish or pickles, making sure to leave at least 2.5 cm/1 in head space.
4. Before placing lids on jars, remove any air pockets in the food using a wooden spoon; *never use metal utensils.*

5. Screw lids tightly on jars and place jars in boiling water. Begin timing when water returns to the boil and process for time specified in recipe.
6. Remove jars with tongs and leave to cool overnight.
7. To make sure that the vacuum has formed, tap the lids lightly with a metal spoon. If you hear a ringing sound, the jar is safely sealed. But if the sound is dull and hollow, you need to reprocess or simply use the condiment right away. Always store jars in a cool, dark spot.

Five Pepper Relish

The combination of sweet red and green peppers, Italian frying peppers, red chilli peppers and black peppercorns make this a colourful, sweet and slightly spicy relish. It's delicious served with curries, hamburgers, hot dogs, barbecued chicken or as a dipping sauce for prawns and raw vegetables. Plan on leaving the relish for about two weeks before serving.

4 medium-sweet red peppers, finely chopped without seeds
4 medium-sweet green peppers, finely chopped without seeds
8 Italian frying peppers, sliced into thin rings without seeds
1 small fresh red chilli pepper, finely chopped with seeds
2 medium onions, finely chopped
225 g/8 oz granulated sugar
175 ml/6 fl oz cider vinegar
1 tablespoon yellow mustard seeds
½ tablespoon black peppercorns

Mix all the ingredients in a large stainless steel saucepan and bring to the boil over a high heat. Reduce the heat and simmer, uncovered, for 6–7 minutes or until the peppers are just tender but still a bit crunchy.

Place the relish into sterilised preserving jars, distributing the liquid evenly, and seal the lid tightly. Process in a boiling water bath for 20 minutes (see pages 129–30 for additional notes on bottling), or allow to cool and refrigerate for two weeks before serving. *Makes about 1 litre/1¾ pints.*

Pear Relish in Raspberry Vinegar

Serve this thick, fruity relish with roast chicken, duck, beef or pork. It's delicious on cottage cheese, hamburgers and on a chicken or turkey sandwich. Try it with a warm duck salad with slivers of pears and almonds in a raspberry vinegar and olive oil dressing.

This relish makes a great Christmas gift. Make it in the autumn when there's a large variety of fresh pears to choose from.

2 large, slightly ripe pears, peeled, cored and coarsely chopped
1 large or 2 small sweet red peppers, chopped
1 medium onion, finely chopped
175 ml/6 fl oz raspberry vinegar
150 g/5 oz granulated sugar
4 tablespoons apple cider vinegar
1 tablespoon yellow mustard seeds
4 peppercorns
2 small dried red chilli peppers
½ teaspoon ground ginger
½ teaspoon salt

Mix all the ingredients in a medium-size stainless steel saucepan. Bring the mixture to the boil over high heat. Reduce the heat and simmer, uncovered, until the relish thickens, about 45 minutes to an hour. Stir the relish frequently to keep it from sticking.

Ladle the hot relish into sterilised preserving jars and seal tightly. Process in a boiling water bath for 15 minutes (see pages 129–30 for additional notes on bottling), or allow to cool and refrigerate for two weeks before serving. *Makes about 250 ml/8 fl oz.*

Cauliflower-Mustard Pickle

This spicy relish is a simplified version of chowchow – an early American favourite. Serve with cold meats, roast chicken, spicy curries, cheese and with antipasto.

1 large cauliflower, broken into small florets
1 litre/1¾ pints cider vinegar
2 tablespoons yellow mustard seeds

½ tablespoon celery seeds
½ tablespoon coriander seeds
50 g/2 oz granulated sugar
40 g/1½ oz plain flour
1½ tablespoons mustard powder
1½ teaspoons ground turmeric
1 medium-size onion, thinly sliced

Place the cauliflower florets in a pan of boiling salted water and boil until slightly tender, about 4–5 minutes. (You want the cauliflower to be *almost* cooked, but not falling apart.) Drain and refresh under cold running water and reserve.

In a large stainless steel pan, mix 750 ml/1¼ pints of the vinegar, the mustard seeds, celery seeds, coriander seeds and sugar. Bring to the boil over a moderately high heat.

Meanwhile, in a medium-size bowl, mix the flour, mustard powder, turmeric and the remaining vinegar to form a smooth paste. Once the vinegar mixture comes to the boil, whisk in the paste, a few tablespoons at a time. Let the vinegar mixture boil for 2–3 minutes.

Place the cauliflower and onion slices into sterilised 450 ml/¾ pint-size preserving jars. Pour the hot vinegar mixture over the vegetables and seal tightly.

Process in a boiling water bath for 20 minutes (see pages 129–30 for additional notes on bottling), or leave to cool and refrigerate for at least two weeks before serving. *Makes about 1.8 litres/3 pints.*

Spicy Cucumber and Pepper Relish

This relish is based on a Tunisian recipe called *Pfepfel bar Labid* (cucumber and pepper relish). I've added hot chilli peppers to give it a spicy bite.

Serve this fresh, simple relish with grilled fish and shellfish, *paella*, curries and salads. Its tart flavour and crunchy texture also complement barbecued meats and chicken.

2 tablespoons fresh lime juice
1 teaspoon salt
1 medium-size cucumber
1 medium-size green pepper, deseeded and chopped
into 2.5 cm/1 in cubes
1 tablespoon thinly sliced hot green chilli pepper

In a serving bowl, mix the lime juice and salt and set aside. Peel the cucumber and slice in half lengthwise. Using the back of a spoon, scoop out the seeds and then slice the cucumber into 1 cm/½ in-wide pieces. Add the cucumber slices and the peppers to the lime juice and salt and stir to coat evenly. Cover and let marinate for about 6 hours before serving. The relish will keep, refrigerated, for about a day or two – after that time it loses its crunchy texture. *Makes about 450 ml/¾ pint.*

Beetroot, Horseradish and Apple Relish

This sharp, slightly spicy relish has a beautiful beetroot-red colour. Serve it with roast chicken, pork, lamb or grilled pork chops. It's also good mixed with soured cream and served with ham, roast beef, beef fondue and grilled fish.

1 large tart red apple, peeled and diced
7.5 cm/3 in piece fresh horseradish root, peeled and sliced into thin strips about 2.5 cm/1 in long
2 small chopped pickled or cooked beetroot, with 3 tablespoons of beetroot juice (see page 136 for recipe for home-made pickled beetroot)
2 tablespoons apple cider vinegar

In a small bowl, mix all the ingredients. Cover and refrigerate for at least 4 hours. Serve within 48 hours. *Makes about 250 ml/8 fl oz.*

Cranberry, Ginger and Grapefruit Relish

This sweet, tart relish is the perfect condiment to serve with roast turkey, duck, goose, chicken or ham.

450 g/1 lb whole cranberries
250 g/9 oz granulated sugar
100 g/4 oz chopped candied ginger in syrup
2 tablespoons syrup from the candied ginger
4 tablespoons grapefruit juice
grated rind from 1 grapefruit
50 g/2 oz flaked almonds

133

In a large saucepan, mix the cranberries, sugar, ginger, syrup, grapefruit juice and rind. Cover and bring to the boil over a high heat. Lower the heat and simmer for 10–15 minutes, or until the cranberries pop open. Remove from the heat and stir in the almonds. Allow to cool and place into sterilised jars. Cover with melted paraffin wax and keep in a dark, cool place. *Makes about 750 ml/1¼ pints.*

Onion and Cassis Relish

Onions and cassis (blackcurrant liqueur) are a wonderful combination. Serve this savoury relish with hamburgers, pâtés, on buttered toast, with pan-fried fish, and with roast chicken or duck.

2 medium-size onions, thinly sliced
175 ml/6 fl oz crème de cassis
4 tablespoons water
40 g/1½ oz brown sugar
2 tablespoons red wine vinegar
4 peppercorns
4 cloves
50 g/2 oz sultanas

Mix all the ingredients, except the sultanas, in a stainless steel saucepan and bring to the boil over a high heat. Reduce the heat and simmer for about 30 minutes, stirring occasionally. Mix in the sultanas, leave to cool, and then refrigerate. The relish will keep for about a week. *Makes about 250 ml/8 fl oz.*

Tomato-Apple Relish

Connie Weeks lives on a farm in Eliot, Maine. There she makes relishes, chutneys, jellies, jam, honey, spins her own wool and makes her own soap. This simple, delicious recipe is one of her best. 'Every gardener has experienced a glut of tomatoes at the end of the gardening season,' she writes in her book, *Using Summer's Bounty – A Country Woman's Source Book.* 'Last year I had not only too many tomatoes, but also many imperfect apples. In scanning recipes for a solution, I came across the following recipe

. . . it makes a sweet relish, an excellent side dish, a fine accompaniment to hamburgers and an interesting addition to a winter salad when fresh vegetables are imported, expensive and often boring.'

1 kg/2 lb peeled, coarsely chopped tomatoes
225 g/8 oz diced tart apples
75 g/3 oz chopped onion
100 g/4 oz chopped celery
2 sweet green peppers, cored and chopped
2 sweet red peppers, cored and chopped
350 ml/12 fl oz cider vinegar
500 g/1¼ lb preserving sugar
1 tablespoon yellow mustard seeds
½ tablespoon whole cloves
1 tablespoon ground cinnamon

Place all the ingredients in a large stainless steel saucepan and cook over a moderate heat for about 2 hours, or until thickened. (Stir the relish occasionally to keep it from sticking to the pan.) Ladle the hot relish into sterilised jars and seal tightly. Process in a boiling water bath for 15 minutes (see pages 129–30 for additional notes on bottling), or leave to cool and place in the refrigerator for a week before serving. *Makes about 1.2 litres/2 pints.*

Jessica's Pickled Oriental Radishes

Pickled radishes are an old Japanese tradition. *Daikon*, a large white Japanese radish, is pickled in a sweet soy mixture and then served with grilled fish.

This is an adaptation of that recipe using ordinary red radishes. It comes from a designer friend, Jessica Weber, of New York.

1 tablespoon sugar
5 tablespoons Japanese soy sauce
1½ tablespoons Oriental sesame oil
2½ tablespoons distilled white vinegar, or Japanese rice wine vinegar
¼ teaspoon hot pepper sauce
30 radishes, washed and trimmed

135

In a medium-size bowl, mix the sugar and soy sauce. Whisk in the oil, vinegar and hot pepper sauce. Score each end of the radishes with an X about 5 mm/⅛ in deep and toss with the marinade. Cover and, tossing occasionally, refrigerate for at least 5 hours and as long as 24 hours. *Makes about 750 ml/1¼ pints.*

Pickled Onions

This recipe makes very authentic-tasting English-style pickled onions. Serve them with cheeses, cold meat platters and pâtés.

1 kg/2 lb small white onions (about 32)
salt
450 ml/¾ pint malt or cider vinegar
1 teaspoon salt
10 cloves
8 black peppercorns
2 bay leaves

Place the onions in a large bowl and cover with boiling water. Leave for about 4 minutes and then drain. Rinse under cold running water and then carefully peel.

Place the peeled onions in a large, shallow tray or roasting pan and sprinkle liberally with salt. Leave overnight. The following day, rinse the onions well and dry thoroughly.

In a large stainless steel pan, heat the vinegar, 1 teaspoon of salt, cloves, peppercorns and bay leaves. Bring the vinegar to the boil over moderately high heat and boil for 5 minutes. Add the onions and bring the vinegar back to the boil. Remove the onions with a slotted spoon and tightly pack into sterilised preserving jars. Pour the hot vinegar over the onions and seal tightly.

Process in a boiling water bath for 30 minutes (see pages 129–30 for additional notes on bottling), or leave to cool and place in the refrigerator for at least two weeks before serving. *Makes about 1.2 litres/2 pints.*

JKR's Pickled Beetroot

These pickles are wonderful. Fresh beetroot and onions are simmered and then pickled in an apple cider vinegar and balsamic vinegar mixture. Serve them with cold meats, cheeses, an antipasto platter or eat them on their own.

$6.99

Sunset

One year — 12 issues now only 3 installments of $6.99 each. You save 40% off the cover price!

Mr/Ms/Mrs _____

(Please Print)   4SQG9

Address _____

_____ Apt.#

City/State/Zip _____

☐ Bill me later   ☐ Payment enclosed

Canada—$33 (includes postage and GST), Mexico—$31, Foreign—$41.
U.S. funds only. Allow 6 to 8 weeks for delivery.

SAVE 40%!

BUSINESS REPLY MAIL
FIRST CLASS MAIL PERMIT NO. 1 MENLO PARK CA

POSTAGE WILL BE PAID BY ADDRESSEE

Sunset

PO BOX 56653
BOULDER CO 80323-6653

24 medium-size beetroot
8 small onions, peeled
600 ml/1 pint apple cider vinegar
120 ml/4 fl oz balsamic, sherry or red wine vinegar
2–4 teaspoons sugar (optional)

Clean the beetroot under cold running water. Place the beetroot in a large pan and cover with water. Boil until *almost* tender when tested with a fork; this will take anything from 15–35 minutes depending on the size and freshness of the beetroot. Remove the beetroot with a slotted spoon (reserving the water), peel and cut in half.

Boil the reserved water; add the onions and boil for 2 minutes. Remove the onions with a slotted spoon (again reserving the water), and cut the onions in half.

In a large stainless steel pan, heat 250 ml/8 fl oz of the reserved water with the apple cider vinegar and balsamic vinegar; add sugar if you want the beetroot to be sweet.

Divide the beetroot and onions equally and place in sterilised, pint-size preserving jars. Ladle the hot vinegar mixture over the beetroot and onions and seal tightly.

Process in a boiling water bath for 30 minutes (see pages 129–30 for additional notes on bottling), or leave to cool and place in the refrigerator for at least two weeks before serving. *Makes about 2 litres/3½ pints.*

Gari: Japanese Pickled Ginger

Gari, pickled fresh ginger, is traditionally served in Japan with *sushi* and *sashimi*. It is said to freshen your breath and cleanse your palate between pieces of raw fish.

Serve about a tablespoon or two of *gari* per person with *sushi* and *sashimi*. It's also delicious served with other Japanese dishes, barbecued meats and chicken, and seafood shish kebab.

225 g/8 oz fresh ginger
1½ tablespoons salt
250 ml/8 fl oz Japanese rice vinegar
120 ml/4 fl oz water
2½ tablespoons sugar

Peel the ginger with a small sharp knife or peeler. Place on a small plate and sprinkle with the salt. Leave overnight.

Rinse the ginger to remove the salt and allow to dry. In a medium-size bowl, mix the vinegar, water and sugar. Add the ginger, cover, and place in the refrigerator or in a cool, dark spot for one to three weeks. The ginger is ready when it turns a subtle pink colour. Slice off a thin piece to see if it's pink throughout.

Remove the ginger from the marinade and place in a small bowl. Cover and refrigerate until ready to serve.

To serve *gari*, use either a sharp knife or a food processor and cut the ginger into paper-thin slices *along* the grain. *Makes about 225 g/8 oz.*

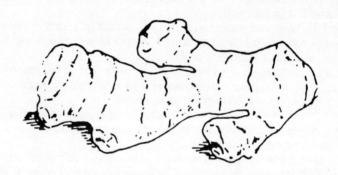

Connie Weeks' Watermelon Rind Pickle

'My family and I have always been fond of this pickle,' writes Connie Weeks, a cook from Eliot, Maine. 'I have never bought a melon just for making the pickle. I always use the rind from our 4th of July, Labor Day and other summertime celebration picnics.' Serve with salads, cold meats, cheese and barbecued chicken.

> 250 g/9 oz watermelon rind pieces, cut into
> 2.5 cm/1 in wide slices (be sure to cut all the dark
> green skin and the red fruit off the pieces of rind)
> 75 g/3 oz salt mixed with 1 litre/1¾ pints water
> 450 ml/¾ pint water
> 450 ml/¾ pint cider vinegar
> 1 kg/2 lb preserving sugar
> 4 cinnamon sticks
> 2 tablespoons whole cloves

138

Place the watermelon rind in a large bowl and cover with the salt water. Place a plate over the bowl and weigh it down with a rock or pie weights in order to keep the rind submerged in the water. Soak in the refrigerator for 12 hours.

Drain the rind and rinse under cold running water. Place the rind in a large pan of boiling water and boil until almost tender when tested with a fork, about 10 minutes. Drain the rind and reserve.

In a large stainless steel pan, mix the water, vinegar, sugar, cinnamon sticks and cloves. Boil over a high heat for 5 minutes. Add the rind and boil about 15–20 minutes, or until the rind is clear. (Be careful not to overcook the rind. Stop cooking as soon as the rind is clear, or it will be mushy.)

Remove the rind with a slotted spoon and fill sterilised preserving jars. Pour the hot vinegar mixture and the spices over the rind and seal tightly. Process in a boiling water bath for 15 minutes (see pages 129–30 for additional notes on bottling), or leave to cool and place in the refrigerator for at least two weeks before serving. *Makes about 1.2 litres/2 pints.*

Kate Slate's Apple Cider Jelly

This is one of those recipes that's too easy to be true. By simply boiling down apple cider, you're left with a naturally sweet, syrupy jelly. Absolutely nothing else is added; the natural sugars and pectin in the apples do all the work. Serve with roast pork or lamb, on top of toast, muffins or ice cream, or with pancakes and waffles.

3.25 litres/6 pints unsweetened apple cider with no additives

In a large, heavy pan, bring the cider to the boil over a high heat. Reduce the heat to moderate and cook the cider at a low, rolling boil until it is reduced to 450 ml/¾ pint, about 2 hours. (Towards the end of the cooking time be sure to watch the jelly. You don't want it to get too thick or it will caramelise. You simply want it to thicken to a jelly-like consistency.)

Pour the hot jelly into a sterilised preserving or jelly jar, close the lid and allow to cool to room temperature. Refrigerate overnight before serving. The jelly will keep, refrigerated, for several months. *Makes about 500 g/1¼ lb.*

Herb-Flavoured Jellies

Making a herb-flavoured jelly can be simple if you follow the recipe above for apple cider jelly. Wrap about 4 tablespoons fresh herbs (rosemary, basil, thyme, sage, marjoram, parsley or a combination) in a double layer of cheesecloth and place in the pot with the cider. Boil the cider until reduced, pressing down on the cheesecloth every now and then to extract the herb flavour. Place a sprig of fresh herb in a sterilised jelly jar and strain the apple cider jelly on top, discarding the cheesecloth. *Makes about 500 g/1¼ lb.*

Apple Cider Jelly with Rose Geranium Leaves

Follow the recipe for apple cider jelly on page 139. Place a clean rose geranium leaf into a sterilised preserving or jelly jar and cover with the hot jelly. The leaf will give the jelly a delicate, but distinctive flavour. *Makes about 500 g/1¼ lb.*

Hot Pepper Apple Cider Jelly

Follow the recipe for apple cider jelly on page 139. Wrap 4 chopped small chilli peppers in a double layer of cheesecloth and place in the pan with the cider. Boil the cider until reduced, pressing down on the cheesecloth every now and then to extract the pepper flavour. Strain the jelly into a sterilised jar and discard the peppers. (The same method can be used to make Apple Cider and Ginger Jelly using a peeled, 5 cm/2 in piece of fresh ginger.) *Makes about 500 g/1¼ lb.*

Red Currant and Mint Jelly

Serve this simple jelly with meats, game and poultry.

275 g/10 oz red currant or blackcurrant jelly
2 tablespoons chopped fresh mint

Mix the jelly and mint in a small saucepan and place over a moderate heat for 2–3 minutes, or until warm and thin. Serve warm or place in the refrigerator, allow to thicken and serve cold. *Makes about 275 g/10 oz.*

8

Chutney

A FRIEND OF MINE recently visited India for the first time and decided to have dinner at one of Bombay's better restaurants. While enjoying a delicious, spicy lamb curry, she innocently asked the waiter to bring a bottle of Major Grey's. He gave her a strange look and said curtly, 'Madam, you'd like some Major who?'

What my friend didn't realise is that commercially made chutneys are frowned upon in India. Although you can find bottled chutneys in some Indian food shops (none of which, by the way, go under the name 'Major Grey's'), almost all Indian chefs and home cooks take a great pride in preparing their own special chutneys. After my friend explained to the waiter what she wanted, he arrived at her table with a huge silver tray filled with a dozen little bowls of freshly made chutneys.

'Chutneys,' writes Santha Rama Rau in the Time-Life book *The Cooking of India*, 'occupy a position of such importance in the food of almost any part of India, and offer such an astonishing diversity of flavours, such a limitless list of ingredients, that a whole book could be written about their uses, possibilities and significance.'

Indian chutneys range from an exotic mixture of grated coconut, tamarind and chilli peppers to fresh mint ground with coriander leaves and lime juice. Their flavour can be hot and spicy or slightly sweet, cool and refreshing. What all chutneys have in common is their ability to wake up the flavours in food and provide contrast in taste and texture to the other foods they are served with.

Most of the chutney that makes its way to American food shops comes via England. The British passion for chutney goes back several hundred years. During the eighteenth century, British civil servants and army officers stationed in India brought bottles of chutney back home with them. The British adored these spicy, exotic concoctions and before long chutney was in great demand. British companies began importing chutney in bulk and sold it under labels like Major Grey's, Colonel Skinner and Bengal Club – all names that evoked the days of the British *raj*.

The popularity of chutney in the United States is more recent, but equally passionate. Major Grey's (which is actually a generic name for a sweet-and-spicy mango chutney) has practically become a household word. It seems that even people who won't have anything to do with Indian food know and love this sweet-and-spicy condiment.

CHUTNEY SURVEY

The word 'chutney' is based on the Hindi word *chatni*, meaning to lick or taste. *The Oxford English Dictionary* defines it as a 'strong relish or condiment compounded of ripe fruits, acids, or sour herbs, and flavoured with chillies, spices, etc', but this simple definition can't capture the many textures and styles of chutney.

Chutneys come from England, India, France and all over the United States; they're made with everything from mangoes and bananas to apples and cucumber. Most of them, I'm sorry to say, are absolutely awful. They are so loaded with sugar and sweeteners that you can barely taste the flavours of all the fruits and spices that went into making them. (It's strange, because it's really so easy to make a good, flavourful chutney; see recipes on pages 143–7.) There are, however, a number of commercially made brands that are delicious.

TASTING NOTES:
Everyone serves chutneys with curries, but there are many other foods that they can complement. Here are just a few ideas:

● Serve a peach chutney on a baked sweet potato or a mango chutney with boiled new potatoes.
● Roast lamb, pork, duck, turkey and chicken are naturals with chutney – either served as a condiment or brushed onto the meat while it's still roasting.
● Chutneys go well with cold meats, cheeses and biscuits.
● Garnish a thick, home-made vegetable stew with a spoonful of peach or a spicy pepper chutney.
● Mix chutneys into sauces and mayonnaise.
● Use chutneys to stuff a tenderloin of pork or a crown roast or a boneless chicken breast.
● Add a spicy chutney to yogurt to make a dip for raw vegetables and crisp-fried Indian breads.
● Serve a fresh, spicy coriander chutney on grilled tomato halves or grilled swordfish or salmon.

- Apple, pear and peach chutneys are delicious served with apple and pumpkin pie.
- Sweet mango chutney makes a fantastic topping for a hot fruit compote.
- One of my favourite sandwiches is thinly sliced brown bread, with thin slices of sharp Cheddar cheese and mango chutney.
- Spread chutney on thin pancakes or inside pitta bread and top with thinly sliced barbecued lamb or grilled steak.
- Chop a few tablespoons of mango and add to devilled eggs.
- Make an apple, peach, pear or mango chutney omelette.

MAKING YOUR OWN CHUTNEYS

Fresh Coriander-Cashew Chutney

This beautiful pale-green chutney is cooling and refreshing, but also spicy. It's a fantastic combination of Indian flavours – fresh coriander leaves blended with cashew nuts, chilli pepper, lemon juice, cumin and yogurt. It takes only minutes to make and is delicious served with grilled chicken, lamb, fish or seafood. It also makes a spicy dip for raw vegetables and fried Indian bread.

4 tablespoons fresh coriander leaves, chopped
1 fresh, small hot green chilli pepper, chopped with seeds
3 tablespoons fresh lemon juice
1 tablespoon water
50 g/2 oz unsalted cashew nuts, chopped
120 ml/4 fl oz plain yogurt
½ teaspoon ground cumin powder
salt and black pepper to taste

Place the coriander, chilli pepper, lemon juice and water in a blender or food processor and blend to form a thick paste. Gradually add the cashews and blend, using a spatula to scrape the mixture down off the sides. Place the paste in a small bowl and mix in the yogurt, cumin and salt and pepper. Place the chutney back in the blender or food processor and blend thoroughly, for about 20 seconds. Place the chutney in a small serving bowl and refrigerate. Serve within 24 hours. *Makes about 200 g/7 oz.*

Fresh Ginger-Coconut Chutney

The fresh, pungent bite of ginger gives this chutney its distinctive flavour. Serve it with curries, rice dishes, grilled meat, chicken and fish or with Chinese stir-fry dishes. The chutney should be made just before serving; if it's refrigerated, it will only keep about a day.

100 g/4 oz peeled and coarsely chopped fresh ginger
25 g/1 oz grated coconut
50 g/2 oz sultanas
4 tablespoons fresh lemon juice
1 clove garlic, chopped
1½ tablespoons coconut milk or water
½ teaspoon salt

Place all the ingredients in a blender or food processor and blend for about 30 seconds. Using a spatula, scrape the mixture down off the sides of the blender and blend for another 45 seconds, or until the mixture forms a thick, chunky purée.
Cover and refrigerate for up to 24 hours. *Makes about 175 g/6 oz.*

Mango Chutney

This chutney has a wonderful balance of sweet and spicy flavours. Serve it with curries, roast duck, chicken and lamb – or just eat it straight out of the jar. You can easily double or triple this recipe and preserve what you can't eat right away.

1 large under-ripe mango, thinly sliced
2 small green peppers, thinly sliced
½ red onion, thinly sliced
1 large fresh green chilli pepper, thinly sliced
75 g/3 oz raisins
120 ml/4 fl oz freshly squeezed grapefruit juice

1 teaspoon grated grapefuit rind
4 tablespoons apple cider vinegar
40 g/1½ oz brown sugar
90 g/3½ oz honey
1½ teaspoons chopped fresh ginger, or ½ teaspoon
dried ground ginger
½ teaspoon yellow mustard seeds
½ teaspoon coriander seeds
¼ teaspoon freshly grated nutmeg

Place all the ingredients in a large stainless steel saucepan and mix well. Let the mixture come to the boil over a high heat. Reduce the heat to low and simmer for about 25 minutes, or until the mixture is thickened and the liquid is syrupy. (If the chutney seems too thin and liquidy, raise the heat to high and let the mixture boil for about 3–4 minutes until slightly thickened.) Place the chutney in hot, sterilised preserving jars and seal tightly. Process for 20 minutes in a boiling water bath (see pages 129–30 for additional notes on bottling), or allow to cool and place in the refrigerator.

Cranberry, Grapefruit, Ginger and Walnut Chutney

This delicious sweet-and-sour chutney has an incredibly beautiful pinkish-maroon colour. The recipe can easily be doubled if you want to make it to give as a Christmas gift.

Serve with roast duck, chicken, turkey or ham, or try it with a turkey or chicken salad or on thin slices of cold ham or roast beef. You could also serve it over vanilla ice cream.

450 g/1 lb whole cranberries
250 ml/8 fl oz grapefruit juice
1 teaspoon grated grapefruit rind
120 ml/4 fl oz apple cider
120 ml/4 fl oz apple cider vinegar
1 small onion, chopped
1 tablespoon minced fresh ginger
1 teaspoon allspice
1 teaspoon ground cinnamon
350 ml/12 fl oz maple syrup (or sugar)
100 g/4 oz chopped walnut halves

In a large stainless steel pan, mix the cranberries, grapefruit juice and rind, apple cider, vinegar, onion, ginger, allspice and cinnamon. Bring the mixture to the boil over a high heat. As soon as it begins to boil, lower the temperature and let the chutney simmer for 10 minutes, uncovered.

Add the maple syrup and, stirring occasionally, let the chutney simmer, uncovered, for 15 minutes or until thickened. Remove from the heat and stir in the walnuts. Let the chutney cool slightly and place in sterilised jars. Cover tightly, leave to cool and refrigerate. Use within two weeks. *Makes about 1.2 litres/2 pints.*

Karen and Judy's Peach-Mango Chutney

Serve with grilled chicken, lamb curry, on a cheese sandwich or with grilled prawns.

750 kg–1 kg/1½–2 lb slightly soft peaches, peeled and coarsely chopped
1 medium-size, slightly soft mango, peeled and coarsely chopped
250 ml/8 fl oz apple cider vinegar
350 g/12 oz honey
120 ml/4 fl oz fresh orange juice
1 clove garlic, minced
1 tablespoon diced fresh ginger
1 teaspoon cinnamon
1 teaspoon cloves
1 teaspoon salt (optional)

Place all the ingredients in a large stainless steel saucepan. Bring the mixture to the boil over a high heat, lower the heat and let simmer, uncovered, for 45 minutes, or until thick. (Be sure to stir the mixture every 10 minutes or so to keep it from sticking.) Place the chutney in hot, sterilised preserving jars and seal tightly. Process for 10 minutes in a boiling water bath (see pages 129–30 for additional notes on bottling), or leave to cool and place in the refrigerator. *Makes about 750 ml/1¼ pints.*

Rhubarb Chutney

Thick, sweet-and-sour, this chutney is based on an old English recipe. It's a great way to preserve the flavour of fresh summer rhubarb. Serve with roast pork, duck or goose, or spread on buttered toast with thinly sliced Cheddar cheese.

1 kg/2 lb fresh rhubarb, cut into small 2.5 cm/1 in pieces
450 g/1 lb white or light brown sugar
150 g/5 oz chopped onion
350 ml/12 fl oz apple cider vinegar
90 g/3½ oz sultanas, coarsely chopped
1 tablespoon chopped fresh ginger
½–1 teaspoon salt
½ teaspoon cayenne pepper
¼ teaspoon ground cinnamon
¼ teaspoon ground cloves

Mix all the ingredients in a large, stainless steel saucepan and place over a moderate heat. Allow to simmer gently for about 40 minutes, or until the mixture is thickened. Remove the saucepan from the heat and leave to stand for 1 hour.

Place the pan over a moderate heat and simmer for an additional 45 minutes. Place the chutney in hot, sterilised jars and seal. Process for 15 minutes in a boiling water bath (see pages 129–30 for additional notes on bottling), or leave to cool and place in the refrigerator. *Makes about 1.25 kg/2½ lb.*

Index

soy, flavoured 114–15
teriyaki 115–16
Vietnamese sweet and
sour fish 118
varieties
fish (South-East Asia)
103–4
hoisin (Chinese barbecue
or Peking) 104–5
lemon (Chinese) 105
oyster (Chinese) 105–6
plum *or* duck (Chinese)
106
satay (Indonesian and
Chinese) 107
Soy
about 107–8
Chinese 109–10
goma (Japanese) 111
Japanese 110
Ketjap manis or *benteng*
(Indonesian) 111
mushroom (Chinese)
112
ponzu (Japanese) 112
sweet-and-sour
(Chinese-American)
113–14
tamari (Japanese-
American) 111
tentsuyu (Japanese) 112
teriyaki (Japanese) 113,
115–16
tonkatsu (Japanese) 114
Orléans process in vinegar
making 29–30
Oyster sauce 105–6, 119

Peach and mango chutney 146
Peanut oil 56–7
Peanut and chilli sauce (*satay*)
116
Peking sauce 104–5
Pepper
black, and wine vinegar 42
cayenne with mustard 17

chilli *see* chilli pepper sauces
vinegar 42
Pickles
about 125–6
beetroot 136–7
cauliflower mustard 131–2
ginger (*gari*) 137–8
onions 136
radishes, oriental 135–6
watermelon rind 138–9
Plum *or* duck sauce 106
Ponzu sauce (Japanese) 112
Pork chops in mustard sauce 26
Prawns sautéed in sesame oil
63

Radishes, pickled 135
Red cabbage soup 47
Red currant and mint jelly 140
Relishes
about 123–5
beetroot, horseradish and
apple 133
cucumber and pepper 132–3
five pepper 130
onion and cassis 134
pear, in raspberry vinegar
131
tomato apple 134–5
Rhubarb chutney 147
Rice vinegars 34–7

Salmon with mustard hazelnut
butter 25
Salsas (Mexican hot pepper
sauce) 71–2
cruda 82
mission style 82–3
picante 81
Sambals (South-East Asian
pepper sauce) 73
Satay (peanut and chilli sauce)
116
Sauces *see* chilli pepper sauces;
horseradish; occidental
sauces; oriental sauces

153

NOW AVAILABLE IN THE
COMET COOKBOOK SERIES